POETRY AND PROSE

BY

JOHN KEATS

A Book of Fresh Verses and New Readings—Essays
and Letters lately found—and Passages
formerly suppressed

EDITED BY H BUXTON FORMAN

AND FORMING
A SUPPLEMENT TO THE LIBRARY EDITION
OF KEATS'S WORKS

LONDON
REEVES & TURNER 196 STRAND
1890

'Tis writ among your childish feats,
　My Guendolen,—when you were " smallish,"
You " helped your father edit Keats "
　By copying those four lines on Dawlish.

" Along the edge " we moved this year,
　Of Devon where our poet stayed,
And wondered whether there or here
　He met his dainty Devon maid.

From Dawlish " over hill and dale
　And bourne " to Teignmouth did we ramble;
Saw Coomb-on-Teign and sweet Coomb Vale
　And Babbicombe,—a rocky scramble!

And Newton Marsh, and close at hand
　Kingsteignton, aye and all the rest,
And drank the beauty of the land
　Wherein the poet wrote his best.

And here you helped me supplement
　The four years' work you saw me finish
Before your childhood's time was spent—
　Before my hair was gray and thinnish.

No matter how you helped me, Guen;
　You " builded better than you knew;"
And now, before I drop the pen,
　I dedicate this book to you.

CONTENTS.

	Page
Fresh Verses and New Readings :—	
New Readings in " Hadst thou liv'd in days of old "	4
New Readings in the EPISTLE TO GEORGE KEATS	4
Cancelled Passages of LAMIA	6
Rejected Stanza and Variations in ISABELLA	10
Rejected Stanza and Variations in THE EVE OF ST. AGNES	14
Variations in the ODE TO A NIGHTINGALE	15
Variations in the ODE TO PSYCHE	15
Variations in FANCY	16
Variations in LINES ON THE MERMAID TAVERN	17
Variation in ROBIN HOOD	17
Cancelled Passages of HYPERION	18
WOMEN, WINE AND SNUFF, additional "Nonsense Verses"	20
New Readings in the HYMN TO APOLLO	21
Variation in the Sonnet "After dark vapors"	21
New Readings in "Unfelt, unheard, unseen"	21
Variation in the SONNET ON THE SEA	22
Variations in "Welcome joy, and welcome sorrow"	22
Variation in the Sonnet "When I have fears"	23
Variations in the SONNET TO HOMER	23
SONNET: THE HUMAN SEASONS, Fresh Version	23
New Readings in LINES ON SEEING A LOCK OF MILTON'S HAIR	24
Variation in the SONNET ON SITTING DOWN TO READ KING LEAR ONCE AGAIN	25
New Readings in the SONNET TO THE NILE	25

viii   CONTENTS.

                                                                  Page
Fresh Verses and New Readings—continued
 New Readings in the Sonnet "Blue! 'Tis the life of
  Heaven" 25
 Variations in "I had a dove" 26
 New Readings in LINES WRITTEN IN THE HIGHLANDS 27
 Cancelled Passage of STAFFA 28
 Variations in the Sonnet "Why did I laugh to-night?" . 29
 Variation in the SONNET ON A DREAM AFTER READING
  DANTE'S EPISODE OF PAULO AND FRANCESCA . . 29
 Variations in SPENSERIAN STANZAS ON CHARLES
  ARMITAGE BROWN 30
 New Readings in the SONG OF FOUR FAERIES . . 30
 AN EXTEMPORE, Episode for a Comic Poem . . . 31
 New Readings in SONNETS ON FAME 34
 Variations in SONNET TO SLEEP 35
 New Readings in LA BELLE DAME SANS MERCI . . 36
 Cancelled Passages of KING STEPHEN 39
 Variations in "Nonsense Verses" on Oxford . . . 44
 Variations in the SONNET TO MRS. REYNOLDS'S CAT . 44
 SONNET TO KEATS ON READING HIS SONNET WRITTEN
  IN CHAUCER, by John Hamilton Reynolds . . . 45
Review of Reynolds's PETER BELL 49
Notice of RETRIBUTION, OR THE CHIEFTAIN'S DAUGHTER,
 a Tragedy 55
Notice of DON GIOVANNI, a Pantomime . . . 61
Fresh Letters and Additional Passages 67
Addenda 181
Index 189

                    FRONTISPIECE.
Portrait of John Hamilton Reynolds: photo-intaglio from a
 miniature by Joseph Severn, kindly lent by Charles
 Green, Esq.

FRESH VERSES AND NEW
READINGS.

FRESH VERSES AND NEW READINGS.

THE Library Edition of Keats's writings published in 1883 was the first serious attempt to bring together in one collection the whole works of Keats in verse and prose and all the most important collateral matter illustrating the works or throwing light upon the career of the man. Of that edition a reissue has been recently called for. In the meantime, the materials for dealing with Keats's works have been considerably enlarged; and to those who possess copies of the original edition it will be advantageous to have in the form of a supplement all the new material, whether in verse or in prose, and the details of all fresh collations of text which it has been possible to make.

To begin, then, with the verse, it will be convenient to give here, in the order in which the poems are arranged in the Library Edition, the results obtained by examining all the fresh material to which I have had access.

Mr. Colvin says in his *Keats* ("English Men of Letters" series, page 223) that, according to an entry in Richard

Woodhouse's Keats Commonplace book, the poem commencing " Hadst thou liv'd in days of old," printed at pages 31 to 33 of the first volume, was "altered from a copy of verses written by K. at the request of his brother George, and by the latter sent as a valentine" to Georgiana Wylie. The valentine, says Woodhouse, began thus :—

>Hadst thou lived in days of old,
>Oh what wonders had been told
>Of thy lively dimpled face,
>And thy footsteps full of grace :
>Of thy hair's luxurious darkling,
>Of thine eyes' expressive sparkling,
>And thy voice's swelling rapture,
>Taking hearts a ready capture.
>Oh ! if thou hadst breathed then,
>Thou hadst made the Muses ten.

This was followed by lines 37 to 68 of the text as printed, and they again by the two couplets—

>Ah me ! whither shall I flee?
>Thou hast metamorphosed me.
>Do not let me sigh and pine,
>Prythee be my valentine.
>
>14 Feby. 1816.

In a second transcript made by George Keats from the Epistle to himself printed at pages 47 to 52, there are some additional variations from the printed text. Line 20 is

>*Glide* from all sorrowing, far, far away :

and in line 45 occurs the expression *just right* in place of *right just*. On the other hand line 77 reads *each moral theme* as in the text, and not *the moral theme* as in George Keats's other copy.

These are the only fresh collations it has been necessary to make in connexion with the volume of 1817: the bulk of the new poetical material relates to the volume of 1820, on the contents of which the above-named manuscript book of Woodhouse's mainly bears. Professor Colvin has allowed me to go through the transcripts in that book,—although I have not thought it necessary to examine those of *The Eve of St. Agnes* and *Hyperion*, seeing that Mr. Colvin had already examined them. In order to deal with the several poems in the sequence given to them in my edition, I must flit from Woodhouse to other authorities and back again: meanwhile, the first thing to note from the Woodhouse book is that there seems to have been some intention of giving the 1820 volume a different title-page from that eventually adopted. On a blank page at the beginning of the book I find sketched in pencil the following:

LAMIA
Hyperion, a Fragment,
ISABELLA
ST. AGNES' EVE,
and other poems.

In the Keats collection of Lord Houghton are two leaves from a draft of Part II of *Lamia*, containing some rejected passages and readings of interest. One page of these fragments begins with line 26,

> When from the slope side of a suburb hill,

and ends with line 49,

> Why will you plead yourself so sad-forlorn

(see Volume II, pages 28 and 29). Between these lines there is a cancelled reading of line 29, namely,

> But left a thought at work in Lycius' head.

Of lines 30 to 33 there are the following readings:

> For the first time since that had been his . . .
> For the first time since he had harbour'd in
> That $\begin{cases} \text{happy Palace} \ldots \\ \text{purple-lined Palace} \ldots \end{cases}$
> For the first time since he soft-harbour'd in
> That purple-lined palace of sweet sin
> Not . . .
> His spirit pass'd beyond its golden bourne
> Into the world . . .
> Into $\begin{cases} \text{the} \\ \text{a} \end{cases}$ busy world almost foresworn.

In line 34 Keats wrote *Lamia* instead of *The Lady*; and line 37 originally began with the words *Of joys devote to him*. In line 39 we read *a minute's thought* instead of *a moment's thought*; and line 40 stands

> Why do you sigh, fair Lamia? said he.

Line 42 has two cancellings, thus—

> You have deserted me ; { I am a ...
> { you mould ...

and line 47 appears thus—

> Wherein he saw himself in Paradise— ...

The passage beginning at

> After the hottest day comes languidest

given in the foot-note at page 30 of Volume II, from the finished manuscript, occurs on the verso of the leaf from which the foregoing extracts are made, and shows some variations, as

> The colour'd eve, half-lidded in the west—

and again

>   for certes they
> Scarcely could tell if this was misery.

In the next line there is a cancelled reading, *said then the youth* for *whisper'd the youth*, and a little lower down *As now I do* stands rejected in favour of *As still I do*. There is also a further variation of line 89, namely

> Of fit sound for this soft ethereal frame.

Lamia's avowal that she had no friends is followed by several cancellings :

> "I have no friends" said␣Lamia␣␣as you list
> Seeing it must be . . .
> Do with your own . . .
> Intreat your many guests.␣␣Then all was was [*sic*] wist

She fell asleep, and Lycius to the shade
Of sleep sunk with her $\begin{Bmatrix} \text{when} \\ \text{dreaming} \end{Bmatrix}$ his fancy stray'd
Into a dream . . .
Of sleep went . . .
Of deep sleep in a moment was betray'd.

The recto of Lord Houghton's other leaf bears the passage beginning with

A haunting music sole perhaps and lone

which was first written

A haunting music lone perhaps and sole

There was some hesitation as to what line 125 should be.

The carved cedar . . .
Sweet cedar carv'd there . . .
Fresh Carved Cedar $\begin{Bmatrix} \text{spread a} \\ \text{mimicking a glade} \end{Bmatrix}$

appear successively. There is a rejected reading for line 129—

On either side a forest they . . .

and another of line 130—

All down the aisled-place—far as the eye could view.

In line 134 *silverly* occurs in place of *silently*; line 135 is wanting; and line 137 stands as follows—

The splendid finish of each nook and niche.

Line 140 reads thus—

Forth $\begin{Bmatrix} \text{creeping} \\ \text{tenderer} \end{Bmatrix}$ imagery of $\begin{Bmatrix} \text{slighter} \\ \text{smaller} \end{Bmatrix}$ trees.

In line 141 *smallest* is cancelled in favour of *in small*, and between that and line 142 occurs the following passage:

> And so till she was sated—then came down
> Soft ligh[t]ing $\begin{Bmatrix} \text{on her head} \\ \text{o'er her Brows} \end{Bmatrix}$ a brilliant crown
> Wreath'd turban-$\begin{Bmatrix} \text{wise} \\ \text{like} \end{Bmatrix}$ of tender wannish fire
> And sprinkled o'er with stars like Ariadne's tiar.

The close of line 144 shows no fewer than four readings rejected in favour of *revels rude*, namely *woeful time*, *woeful day*, *time of woe*, and *day of woe*, each of which, preferable in itself to the reading adopted, must have had to give place on account of the exigencies of rhyme. Of the next couplet, however, the received text is a great improvement on the draft, which reads

> The day came soon and all the gossip-rout
> O senseless Lycius   Dolt! Fool! Madman! Lout!

On the verso of the leaf occur lines 191 to 198 with cancellings, thus—

> When in an antichamber every guest
> With fragrant oils his . . .
> When in an antichamber every guest
> Tended by ministering slaves nis . . .
> When in an antichamber every guest
> Had $\begin{Bmatrix} \text{felt} \\ \text{had} \end{Bmatrix}$ the cold full sponge to pleasure press'd.

In lines 195 and 196 occurs the rejected reading,

> they all to banquet came
> In white robes hymeneal.

10   FRESH VERSES AND NEW READINGS.

In the Woodhouse book is a transcript from an autograph manuscript of *Isabella*, with notes and corrections, some in the poet's writing and some in other handwritings. It is almost safe to assume that any variation of Woodhouse's version from the printed text is a genuine reading incidental to the stage of the composition which had been reached when the holograph was transcribed. The first variation is in stanza I, the sixth line of which reads thus—

> It soothed each to be each other by,

and line 6 of stanza IV first stood

> Lorenzo, if thy tongue speak not love's tune.

Afterwards *lips breathe* was substituted for *tongue speak*. Opposite the close of stanza VI, Keats has written in pencil "Stop this as you please." Stanza VII originally closed with a different couplet from that of the published text and was followed by a stanza which has not, I believe, been printed. The change of couplet and erasure of the stanza are among Keats's master-strokes of cunning craftsmanship: here are the ten cancelled lines :—

> "Lorenzo, I would clip my ringlet hair
> To make thee laugh again and debonnair."
>
> "Then should I be," said he, "full deified;
>   And yet I would not have it, clip it not:
> For, lady, I do love it where 'tis tied
>   About the neck I dote on, and that spot

> That anxious dimple it doth take a pride
>   To play about.—Ay, lady, I have got
> Its shadow in my heart, and every sweet
> Its mistress owns there summed all complete.

It will be remembered that instead of all this we have the admirable couplet,

> "Lorenzo"—here she ceas'd her timid quest,
> But in her tone and look he read the rest.

The reading "many once proud-quiver'd loins" of the text (stanza XIV, Volume II, page 49), with its intrusive-looking hyphen, has no support from this manuscript; and I am disposed to think the hyphen should disappear, so as to leave the sense many loins once proud, now quivered (for quivering), which would be characteristic though not strictly defensible. The epithet *proud-quiver'd*, as an equivalent to *bearing proud quivers (of arrows)*, does not commend itself to me as what Keats meant, though of course it may be. The first line of stanza XIX was originally

> O eloquent Boccace of green Arno!

and the final couplet was a rhymeless one—

> For venturing one word unseemly mean,
> In such a place, on such a daring theme.

For these three lines the published version stands substituted in Keats's writing. The couplet of stanza XX was originally written as published; but Keats substituted for the first line of it

> Thy Muse's Vicar in the english tongue;

and afterwards rejected that for the original reading. In the fifth line of stanza XXIV Woodhouse has *courteous* in place of *courteously*. He had left a blank for the couplet of stanza XXV, presumably finding the original unfinished in that particular. Keats inserted the couplet

> When, looking up, he saw her features fair
> Smile through an indoor lattice, debonair.

Someone, probably Taylor, took exception to this, and suggested

> When lo an indoor lattice met his view,
> And her fair features smiling playful through.

Keats, ever modest with his friends, altered his own couplet to that of the text—

> When, looking up, he saw her features bright
> Smile through an indoor lattice, all delight.

Apropos of the word *debonair*, he added the note—"As I have used this word before in the poem you may use your judgement between your lines and mine.—I think my last alteration will do." This would seem to indicate that, at that stage in the proceedings, he had not thought of altering the couplet of stanza VII and striking out the original stanza VIII. The eighth line of stanza XXXVIII reads

> And it shall turn a diamond in the tomb.

In the third line of stanza XL *heaven of a kiss* is cancelled in favour of *taste of earthly bliss.* In stanza XLIV, line 3, we read *campaign* for *champaign.* In stanza XLVII, lines 5 and 6 were written as in the text—

> And freezes utterly unto the bone
> Those dainties made to still an infant's cries;

Keats struck out line 6 and substituted *Love's sighful throne* for *unto the bone,* without completing the revision; but the original reading is marked by another hand for restoration. Line 6 of stanza XLVIII originally stood thus—

> Three hoürs were they at this travail sore;

this is altered in Keats's hand to

> Three hours they labour'd at this travail sore;

presumably because someone objected to *hours* being made to do duty for two syllables, and failed to observe that *labour'd* and *labouring* both came into the stanza as revised. Stanza L opened thus—

> With duller sliver than the Persean sword
>   They cut away—no foul Medusa's head
> But one's . . .

and the published reading was substituted in Keats's writing, save the elimination of the possessive *s* from the last word. The sixth line of the stanza was originally

> If ever any piece of love was dead,

and this is the last variation noticeable in the Woodhouse copy. At the close are inscribed the words "Written at Teignmouth in the Spring of 1818 at the suggestion of J. H. R."

Of *The Eve of St. Agnes* (Volume II, pages 71 to 105) we have now what is almost as good for critical uses as the missing holograph of the first seven stanzas. As a result of examining the relative portion of Woodhouse's transcript of this poem, Mr. Colvin gives (*Keats*, pages 229-30) "the following table of the changes in those stanzas made by the poet in the course of composition :—

"Stanza I. : line 1, for 'chill' stood 'cold': line 4, for 'was' stood 'were': line 7, for 'from' stood 'in': line 9 (and Stanza II., line 1), for 'prayer' stood 'prayers'. Stanza III. : line 7, for 'went' stood 'turn'd': line 8, for 'Rough' stood 'Black'. After Stanza III. stood the following Stanza, suppressed in the poem as printed.

4.
> But there are ears may hear sweet melodies,
> And there are eyes to brighten festivals,
> And there are feet for nimble minstrelsies,
> And many a lip that for the red wine calls—
> Follow, then follow to the illumined halls,
> Follow me youth—and leave the eremite—

> Give him a tear—then trophied bannerals
> And many a brilliant tasseling of light
> Shall droop from arched ways this high baronial night.

"Stanza V.: line 1, for 'revelry' stood 'revellers': lines 3-5, for—

> 'Numerous as shadows haunting fairily
> The brain new-stuff'd in youth with triumphs gay
> Of old romance. These let us wish away,'—

stood the following :—

> 'Ah what are they? the idle pulse scarce stirs,
> The muse should never make the spirit gay;
> Away, bright dulness, laughing fools away.'"

Woodhouse dates the *Ode to a Nightingale* "May 1819", as in the Dilke manuscript. I find in stanza 5 of his transcript, line 1, an unnoted variation—*tell* for *see*; line 2 of stanza 8 reads

> To toll me back from thee unto myself,

and it should perhaps be mentioned that the word *away* does not occur in the last line of stanza 2. See foot-note 2, pages 110-11, Volume II.

A consultation of the holograph of the journal-letter of February-May 1819, in which a considerable mass of poetry was transcribed by Keats for his brother and sister-in-law, yields some fresh readings of the *Ode to Psyche* (Volume II, pages 119 to 121): line 6 has *awaked* in place of *awaken'd*; line 10 *whisp'ring fan* for *whisp'ring roof*, which is a curious instance of a rhyme deliberately lost; line 14 stands thus—

> Blue, freckle-pink, and budded Syrian

and the word *Syrian* is quite unequivocally written in lieu of *Tyrian*. Line 23 is a question—

> His Psyche true?

instead of an emphatic answer—

> His Psyche true!

In line 28 we read *hadst* for *hast*, and in line 36 *O Bloomiest!* for *O brightest!* Line 44 begins with *O* instead of *So*; in line 57 *charmed* stands cancelled for *lull'd*, and in line 62 *frame* for *feign*. At the close of this wonderful piece of work Keats has written in modest playfulness

> Here endethe ye Ode to Psyche.

The manuscript of the journal-letter to George Keats and his wife, written in the winter of 1818-19, includes a copy of the poem entitled *Fancy* (Volume II, pages 122 to 126). This copy corresponds generally with that from which the variations are given in Volume II. The principal variations which it remains to give from the letter are—*vesper from the sky* in line 24; *then* for *there* in line 25; in place of lines 33 and 34

> All the faery buds of May
> On spring turf or scented spray;

creep for *peep* in line 55; and *too oft and oft* for *so very oft* in line 76.

In the same letter is a transcript of "Bards of Passion

"BARDS OF PASSION"—MERMAID TAVERN.

and of Mirth" (Volume II, pages 127 to 129). This Keats seems to have copied into his letter from the original manuscript written in his Beaumont and Fletcher, with but little variation. The line which stands next to line 30 in the Beaumont and Fletcher, and is mutilated, turns out to be

> They must sojourn with their cares;

so that he seems to have failed to discover the want of a rhyme even while writing the poem a second time.

In the *Lines on the Mermaid Tavern* (Volume II, page 130) Woodhouse reads *booze* for *bowse* in line 11, *new old sign* without any hyphen in line 19, and the last four lines as in the Dilke manuscript. His transcript of *Robin Hood* shows the following variation in line 25 (Volume II, page 134)—

> Never any of the clan

and gives the date as 3 February 1819, which is of course a clerical error for 1818: Reynolds's sonnets, to which the poem is a reply, are recorded in the next page of Woodhouse's book as having appeared in the *Yellow Dwarf* for the 21st of February 1818.

Woodhouse appears to have had copied into his Commonplace book the manuscript of *Hyperion* before it was revised finally for the impression of 1820, and to have marked in pencil the subsequent omissions and alterations. The transcript is said by Mr. Colvin (*Keats*, page 231) to show the following variations:

18   FRESH VERSES AND NEW READINGS.

"Book I. After line 21 stood the cancelled lines—

> 'Thus the old Eagle, drowsy with great grief,
> Sat moulting his weak plumage, never more
> To be restored or soar against the sun;
> While his three sons upon Olympus stood.'

In line 30, for 'stay'd Ixion's wheel' stood 'eased Ixion's toil'. In line 48, for 'tone' stood 'tune'. In line 76, for 'gradual' stood 'sudden'. In line 102, after the word 'Saturn,' stood the cancelled words—

> 'What dost think?
> Am I that same? O Chaos!'

In line 156, for 'yielded like the mist' stood 'gave to them like mist'. In line 189, for 'Savour of poisonous brass' stood 'A poison-feel of brass'. In line 200 for 'When earthquakes jar their battlements and towers' stood 'When an earthquake hath shook their city towers.' After line 205 stood the cancelled line 'Most like a rose-bud to a fairy's lute.' In line 209, for 'And like a rose' stood 'Yes, like a rose.' In line 268, for 'Suddenly' stood 'And, sudden.'

"Book II. In line 128, for 'vibrating' stood 'vibrated.' In line 134 for 'starry Uranus' stood 'starr'd Uranus' (some friend doubtless called Keats's attention to the false quantity).

"Book III. After line 125 stood the cancelled lines:—

> 'Into a hue more roseate than sweet pain
> Gives to a ravish'd nymph, when her warm tears
> Gush luscious with no sob; or more severe.'

In line 126, for 'most like' stood 'more like.'"

The unfinished line and sentence with which the fragment of *Hyperion* closes is filled up in pencil in the Woodhouse transcript, wherein we read

>   At length
> Apollo shriek'd—and lo from all his limbs
> Celestial Glory b~~rake~~ dawn'd : he was a god !

The words may be confidently attributed to Keats; and it must be assumed that he deliberately preferred to let the fragment, as given to the public, end abruptly, as it does at page 177 of Volume II, with the word *Celestial*. Apart from the fineness of the recovered line, it is interesting to learn that the fragment did not end, at all events, with one of the "too many Miltonic inversions" which led Keats to abandon the undertaking. The conclusion which he published,—

> Apollo shriek'd ;—and lo ! from all his limbs
> Celestial   *   *   *   *   *   *
>   *   *   *   *   *   *   *   *

was certain to leave the impression that the poet was about to tell something concerning all the celestial limbs of Apollo. As the adjective clearly belongs to the suppressed noun *glory*, the only natural impression was a false one.

Mr. Colvin (*Keats*, page 185) gives an extract from Charles Armitage Brown's manuscript memoir of Keats, in Lord Houghton's collection, showing that *Hyperion, a Vision*, was not after all an early version. It is quite positively and unmistakably recorded that, during November and December 1819, Keats " was deeply engaged in remodelling the fragment of *Hyperion* into the form of a Vision." The evidence of Brown is not to be disputed; but it is stated that Woodhouse, in a book now destroyed by fire, left a similar record. Notwithstanding the beauty of isolated passages in the Vision, nothing could be much sadder than the distinct degradation to which Keats, with his powers undermined by disease, submitted the noble fragment *Hyperion*. Here are textual changes so much the reverse of improvements as to show decay of artistic faculty; but the saddest evidence of such decay is in the impracticable scheme whereby the simple grandeur of the narrative is transmuted into the hopeless complexity of a vision witnessed by the poet with a quasi-classic conductress.

The following couplets, which were preserved by Keats's fellow medical student Henry Stephens, were sent to me by Mr. W. H. Doeg, too late for insertion in their proper place, among the early poems:

WOMEN, WINE AND SNUFF.

Give me women, wine and snuff
Until I cry out " hold, enough !"
You may do so sans objection
Till the day of resurrection;
For bless my beard they aye shall be
My beloved Trinity.

The *Hymn to Apollo* (Volume II, pages 208-9) is

headed *Fragment of an Ode to Apollo* in Woodhouse's book. In the sixth line of stanza 1 he reads *Round* for *Of*, and in the eleventh line *low-creeping* for *low crawling*. In stanza 2, line 8 reads

> Oh! why didst *Thou* pity, and beg for a worm?

In the eleventh line of that stanza, *I not* stands for *not I*. In stanza 3, line 3, *in earth* stands for *in the Earth*; and line 8 reads thus—

> To tie for a moment thy plant round his brow,— . . .

Woodhouse gives the 31st of January 1817 as the date of the Sonnet "After dark vapors" (Volume II, page 216), reading the fifth line thus—

> The anxious mouth relieving from its pains

and the word *mouth* is very plainly written instead of *month*.

Of a manuscript draft of the Lines beginning "Unfelt, unheard, unseen," (Volume II, pages 226-7) there is a fac-simile in the American edition of 1883, showing several revisions of text. The third line of Stanza 1 seems to have been intended to end with *dying* and then with *kissing*; and there is a cancelled line 4 which appears to have been

> And stifling up $\left\{ {\text{the} \atop \text{all}} \right\}$ touch . . .

Stanza 2 shows a cancelled opening—

How sleek those faery lids

How moist $\left\{\begin{array}{c}\text{that}\\\text{the}\end{array}\right\}$ lip that bids

E'en in . . .

The fourth line in the stanza originally opened with

E'en in their quiet stillness

and the final line of the stanza was

That every Joy and Grief and Feeling drowns.

This is struck out in favour of

How Love doth know no fulness nor no bounds.

It is noteworthy here how the artist comes out even in the elaboration of such a trifle as this. The quotation substituted for the weak original line with its bad rhyme made the poem beautiful. There are two cancelled openings for Stanza 3—

So that my sight is dim

and

And so no faults nor flaws.

Woodhouse records that the Sonnet on the Sea (Volume II, page 228) was published in *The Champion* for the 17th of August 1817; and he reads *where* for *whence* in line 7—no doubt correctly. In the Fragment "Welcome joy, and welcome sorrow" (Volume II, pages 234-5) he reads *flames burn under* in line 6, *storm-wreck'd* for *shipwreck'd* in line 13, and *aspics* for *aspic* in line 17. The date of the Sonnet "When I have fears" (Volume II, page 236) he gives as

February 1818; and he reads *feel* for *think* in line 7. In the Sonnet to Homer (page 237) he gives the fifth and sixth lines thus :—

> So wast thou blind ; but then the veil was rent,
> And Jove uncurtain'd heaven to let thee live, . . .

He merely dates the sonnet 1818. In his copy of the letter to Bailey written from Teignmouth in September 1818, the Sonnet entitled *The Human Seasons* (Volume II, pages 247-8) appears with very interesting variations. Indeed there is scarcely a line, after the first, identical with the published text ; and it will be best to transcribe the version entire :

> Four seasons fill the measure of the year;
> Four seasons are there in the mind of Man.
> He hath his lusty Spring, when Fancy clear
> Takes in all beauty with an easy span :
> He hath his Summer, when luxuriously
> He chews the honied cud of fair spring thoughts,
> Till in his soul, dissolv'd, they come to be
> Part of himself : He hath his Autumn Ports
> And havens of repose, when his tired wings
> Are folded up, and he content to look
> On mists in idleness : to let fair things
> Pass by unheeded as a threshhold brook.
> He hath his winter too of Pale misfeature,
> Or else he would forget his mortal nature.

Concerning the *Lines on seeing a Lock of Milton's Hair*, Keats has recorded that he wrote them "at Hunt's, at his request." In the foot-note at pages 249-50 of Volume II, mention is made of three manuscripts, neither of which could be the original done at Hunt's. On looking over some manuscripts of Hunt's, I have lately found, in one of those commonplace-books wherein he wrote and rewrote his poems piece-meal, what seems to be the actual start made by Keats in pursuance of his friend's request. Perhaps that request was accompanied by an encouraging "Here's a note-book, Keats; go on!" At all events, here, between two pages of Hunt's own poetry, are the first seventeen lines of Keats's poem, commencing with a false start, *Father of*, rejected for "Chief of organic numbers". The sixth and seventh lines are clearly meant to read

> Ah what a mad endeavour
> Maketh he . . ,

but *mad* is badly written, and *Maketh* is written *Macketh* (not *Worketh*). Of line 12 there is a cancelled reading—

> O living fane of Sounds—

which is much better than

> Live temple of sweet noise

but had to be rejected on account of the jingle created by *sounds* and *soundest*. Line 17 is

> Lend thine ear!

closed with a note of exclamation; so that the carrying on the sense to what follows in the text was an afterthought. With this line the fragment ends, though

MILTON'S HAIR—KING LEAR—BLUE.

Keats had but to turn over one leaf for another blank page.

In the Sonnet *On sitting down to read King Lear once again* (Volume II, pages 252-3), Woodhouse gives in his transcript only one variation not previously recorded—namely *this* for *our* in line 10. He records the 6th of February 1818 as the date of the Sonnet to the Nile (Volume II, page 254), and is thus at variance by two days with Keats's own statement. Lines 6 to 8 he transcribed thus:

> Art thou so beautiful, or a wan smile
> Pleasant but to those men who, sick with toil,
> Rest them a space 'twixt Cairo and Dekan?

Line 10 appears as

> And ignorance doth make a barren waste . . .

A manuscript of the Sonnet on blue, written in answer to one of Reynolds's on dark eyes (Volume II, pages 257-8), found its way to America; and a so-called facsimile of it, now shorn of its first line, appeared in *The Century Guild Hobby Horse* for July 1886. Line 6 and those following it seem to have exercised the poet a good deal. Mr. Horwood's variation is not shown by this copy; but, as far as the *Hobby Horse* reproduction is legible, the intentions seem to have been as follows:—

And all his vassal streams ; { Pools numberless / Lakes, Waterfalls / Lakes, Pools and Seas

And Waterfalls and Fountains never ran

Or $\left\{\begin{array}{c}\text{well'd}\\\text{flow'd}\end{array}\right\}$ or slept but still . . .

Line 8 stands thus—

Subside but to a dark blue Nativeness.

Line 11 originally opened with *The Violet*; line 12 shows the curious noun *Hiddenness*, struck out in favour of *Secrecy*; in line 13 *then how high* is cancelled for *But how great*; and line 14 originally began with the word *Trembling*. Woodhouse's transcript of the sonnet corresponds verbally with the text of this edition: he gives the date as the 8th of February 1818.

The journal-letter of 1818-19 to George and Georgiana Keats contains a copy of the little Song " I had a dove" (Volume II, page 281). In this copy the third line is

O what could it mourn for? it was tied . . .

Line 5 reads *did* for *should*, line 6 *would* for *should* and *dove* for *bird*, line 7 *on* for *in*, and line 8 *could* for *would*.

Woodhouse gives the Sonnet *To a Lady seen for a few Moments at Vauxhall* as at page 282 of Volume II, supplying, however, the date, 4 February 1818.

Since 1883 I have found in *The Examiner* for the 14th of July 1822 a complete text of the Lines written in the Highlands, which occupy pages 299 to 302 of the second volume of this edition. *The Examiner* gives them the title *Lines Written in the Scotch Highlands*, mentions that portions of the poem had appeared in " a late

LINES WRITTEN IN THE HIGHLANDS.

Number of the *New Monthly Magazine*," and that it was forwarded to the editor of that magazine entire. The text corresponds throughout with that which I have given, save in line 5, which contains the words "in days of old" instead of "by times of old," and in the matter of punctuation. The *Examiner* version is full of notes of exclamation.

In Lord Houghton's collection is a holograph manuscript of the poem, at the end of which Keats has written the title as given in this edition. The first line shows a rejected reading, thus:

> There is a charm in footing slow across a { silent plain / grand camp ... }

I suppose the cancelled *grand camp* would have been *grand campaign* if Keats had not thought better of it before finishing the line. Line 2 ends with *when glory had the gain*, not *where*. Lord Houghton's readings in lines 2, 4, and 5 (see foot-note, page 300) are not borne out by the manuscript. Line 5 was originally written

> In every spot there is a joy made known by times of old

but the words *In every spot* and *there is a joy* are marked for transposition. In line 10 Keats clearly wrote *scurf*, not *surf*. Line 13 shows the cancelled reading *Blue hether bells* for *Light heather bells*, and line 16 *from travels drear* for *on travels drear*. In line 21 *keeps* is rejected in favour of *is*. Line 23 shows no trace of the reading *World* for *Soul* which I regarded as an error of transcription in the Dilke manuscript. In line 25 *a* is substituted for *the* before *Madman*; and in line 27 *many a Man* is rejected for *many a one*. Line 29 originally began with *Short is the hour* instead of *Scanty the hour*. In line 35 *one* is written by mistake for *on*. The first word of line 38 was originally *Hair*, but was altered to *Locks*; and line 44 originally opened with *Upon its marble diadem,—its* being struck out for *rough*. In line 45 *the anchor* and *our anchor* are rejected in favour of *his anchor*; but the next line shows no trace of the preposition *in* substituted for *on* by Lord Houghton.

In 1883 I hazarded the conjecture that line 50 of *Staffa* (Volume II, page 311) should end with *grace* instead of *glance*, so as to rhyme with line 49, which ends with *place*. In the *Life, Letters* &c., where the poem first appeared, and in the current editions, the lines stand without any indication of a hiatus to account for the lack of rhyme. Mr. Colvin has found the explanation of this defect in Woodhouse's Commonplace book, containing transcripts of the chief part of Keats's poems unpublished in 1819: "some contain gaps which Woodhouse has filled up in pencil from later drafts: to others are added corrections, or suggestions for corrections, some made in the hand of Mr. Taylor and some in that of Keats himself." In that book, *Staffa* is continued thus in pencil after line 49 :—

> 'Tis now free to stupid face,
> To cutters, and to Fashion boats,
> To cravats and to petticoats :—

> The great sea shall war it down,
> For its fame shall not be blown
> At each farthing Quadrille dance.
> So saying with a spirit's glance
> He dived.

Perhaps Keats forgot when he wrote the six doggerel lines that Lycidas was the spokesman; saw the incongruity when he copied the verses; but did not think them worth mending further than by excision. The holograph letter contains the doggerel lines, but in line 45 the epithet is *stupid*, not *dullèd*. The circumstances do not warrant the restoration of the doggerel lines to the text.

The Sonnet "Why did I laugh to-night?" (Volume II, page 333) being one of those transcribed by Keats in his journal-letter of February-May 1819, I have been able to consult the holograph, in which the sixth line begins with "Say, wherefore did I laugh?" instead of "I say, why did I laugh?"—while the eleventh line reads *could* for *would*. Of the Sonnet on *A Dream, after reading Dante's Episode of Paulo and Francesca* (Volume II, pages 334-5) the manuscript which forms part of the same journal-letter shows no new reading beyond the inferior word *in* for *'mid* in the tenth line. Woodhouse's record confirms my conjecture that that sonnet was composed in April 1819.

The *Spenserian Stanzas on Charles Armitage Brown* (Volume II, pages 337-8) as given in the holograph letter of February-May 1819 show one or two variations from the printed text. In lines 3 and 4 we find the reading

> As hath the seeded thistle when in parle
> It holds the zephyr,

which should probably take its place in the text; and so no doubt should *hoarse* for *brave* in line 5 of stanza 3.

The Sonnet "If by dull rhymes" (Volume II, page 339) also occurs in this journal-letter; but the holograph is imperfect, ending abruptly with line 4, and showing no variation from the printed text of the sonnet. The *Song of Four Faeries* (Volume II, pages 340 to 344) is all there, without any account being given of the composition. In line 9 is the cancelled reading *Ever beat* for *Faintless* (not *Faintly*) *fan*; line 19 reads *my skies* for *their skies*; lines 23, 29, and 30 read *Spright* for *Spirit*; line 26 shows a cancelled reading, *and studded* for *all studded*; line 32 has *sedge shaded* for *sedge-bury'd*; of line 35 there is the cancelled reading

> Where the flowers amid sweet troubles;

line 40 appears to have begun originally with *For in sooth I'm* instead of *Soothly I am*; line 46 stands as

> Far beyond the search and quest;

in line 53 *brightness* is cancelled in favour of *brilliance*; in line 55 *of* is written by mistake instead of *for*; line 65 originally began with

> Chillier than the water;

lines 69 and 70 are

> Shall we leave them and go seek
> Couches warm as their's is cold ;

line 80 reads *Spright* for *Sprite*; there is a rejected variation of line 82, namely

> To the very torrid fountains—

and another which is too well obliterated to be read securely; the word *the* is left out of line 89, probably by accident; after line 91 are the cancelled lines

> Let us fly
> Ah my love, my life ;

and in line 98 *where* stands in place of *when*.

The holograph of this same journal-letter of February-May 1819 contains among its varieties and novelties ninety-six lines of verse purporting to be an *extempore*. Mr. Colvin (*Macmillan's Magazine,* August 1888) regards them as being connected in some sort with the *Song of Four Faeries* to which I have just referred; and certainly they are trivial enough for such a connexion. Here, at all events, they are,—with no particular reason for commencing, and only a little more for ending, beyond the one stated in prose at the conclusion :—

> When they were come into the Faery's Court
> They rang—no one at home—all gone to sport
> And dance and kiss and love as faerys do
> For Faries be as humans lovers true—
> Amid the woods they were so lone and wild
> Where even the Robin feels himself exil'd
> And where the very brooks as if afraid

Hurry along to some less magic shade.
'No one at home'! the fretful princess cry'd
'And all for nothing such a dre[a]ry ride
And all for nothing my new diamond cross
No one to see my persian feathers toss
No one to see my Ape, my Dwarf, my Fool
Or how I pace my Otaheitan mule.
Ape, Dwarf and Fool why stand you gaping there
Burst the door open, quick—or I declare
I'll switch you soundly and in pieces tear'.
The Dwarf began to tremble and the Ape
Star'd at the Fool, the Fool was all agape
The Princess grasp'd her switch but just in time
The dwarf with piteous face began to rhyme.
" O mighty Princess did you ne'er hear tell
What your poor servants know but too too well
Know you the three great crimes in faery land
The first alas! poor Dwarf I understand
I made a whipstock of a faery's wand
The next is snoring in their company
The next the last the direst of the three
Is making free when they are not at home.
I was a Prince—a baby prince—my doom
You see, I made a whipstock of a wand
My top has henceforth slept in faery land.
He was a Prince the Fool, a grown up Prince
But he has never been a King's son since
He fell a snoring at a faery Ball—
Your poor Ape was a Prince and he poor thing
Picklock'd a faery's boudour—now no king
But ape—so pray your highness stay awhile
'Tis sooth indeed we know it to our sorrow—
Persist and *you* may be an ape tomorrow—
While the Dwarf spake the Princess all for spite
Peal'd the brown hazel twig to lilly white
Clench'd her small teeth, and held her lips apart

Try'd to look unconcern'd with beating heart.
They saw her highness had made up her mind
And quaver'd like the reeds before the wind
And they had had it, but O happy chance
The Ape for very fear began to dance
And grin'd as all his ugliness did ache—
She staid her vixen fingers for his sake
He was so very ugly : then she took
Her pocket ~~glass~~ mirror and began to look
First at herself and [then] at him and then
She smil'd at her own beauteous face again.
Yet for all this—for all her pretty face
She took it in her head to see the place.
Women gain little from experience
Either in Lovers, husbands or expense.
The more the beauty the more fortune too
Beauty before the wide world never knew.
So each fair reasons—tho' it oft miscarries.
She thought *her* pretty face would please the faries.
"My darling Ape I wont whip you today
Give me the Picklock sirrah and go play."
They all three wept—but counsel was as vain
As crying cup biddy to drops of rain.
Yet lingeringly did the sad Ape forth draw
The Picklock from the Pocket in his Jaw.
The Princess took it and dismounting straight
Trip'd in blue silver'd slippers to the gate
      full
And touch'd the wards, the Door ~~opes~~ cou[r]teou[s]ly
Opened—she enter'd with her servants three.
Again it clos'd and there was nothing seen
But the Mule grasing on the herbage green.

   End of Canto xii

   Canto the xiii

The Mule no sooner saw himself alone

Than he prick'd up his Ears—and said 'well done
At least unhappy Prince I may be free—
No more a Princess shall side saddle me
O King of Othaietè—tho' a Mule
'Aye every inch a King'—tho 'Fortune's fool'
Well done—for by what Mr Dwarfy said
I would not give a sixpence for her head'.
Even as he spake he trotted in high glee
To the knotty side of an old Pollard tree
And rub['d] his sides against the mossed bark
Till his Girths burst and left him naked stark
Except his Bridle—how get rid of that
Buckled and tied with many a twist and plait.
At last it struck him to pretend to sleep
And then the thievish Monkies down would creep
And filch the unpleasant trammels quite away.
No sooner thought of than adown he lay
Sham'd a good snore—the Monkey-men descended
And whom they thought to injure they befriended.
They hung his Bridle on a topmost bough
And of[f] he went run, trot, or anyhow—
Brown is gone to bed—and I am tired of rhyming— . . .

For the proper context see later on, pages 146 and 147.

The two Sonnets on Fame (Volume II, pages 345-6) occur in the same journal-letter, but reversed in order. Of the one commencing with the words "Fame, like a wayward girl," the holograph shows scarcely any variation, though line 12 reads *Ye lovelorn Artists* for *Ye Artists lovelorn*. The other Sonnet opens with *How is that Man misled*, altered to *How fever'd is that Man*; lines 7 and 8 are

> As if a clear Lake meddling with itself
> Should cloud its pureness with a muddy gloom;

and lines 13 and 14 show the cancelled reading

> Why then should man his own bright name deface
> And burn our pleasures in his selfish fire.

The fourteenth line is left standing thus—

> Spoil his salvation *by* a fierce miscreed?

instead of *for a fierce miscreed*.

These sonnets are followed by that to Sleep (Volume II, pages 347-8), of which the copy so sent to George Keats corresponds almost exactly with the printed text, reading, however, *dewy Charities* for *lulling charities* in line 8. In line 12 *like the mole* has been rejected in favour of *like a mole*.

Among all the new material which has come to light since the first issue of this edition of Keats's writings, there is little if anything that exceeds in interest that part of the journal-letter written in the spring of 1819 which includes a copy of *La Belle Dame sans Merci*. This poem I had placed tentatively at the close of Keats's poetic career, adopting in the text the version printed during his life-time in *The Indicator*. The holograph now brought to light has no bearing on the text; but it leaves no doubt that this wonderful poem was composed in the spring of 1819; and, had the information come to light soon enough, I should of course have placed *La Belle Dame* a few pages earlier in the volume. This copy shows many corrections, and is clearly a very early one, though not, I should say, the first. It accounts for most of the readings which distinguish Lord Houghton's version of the poem from the more authoritative one of *The Indicator*, and confirms my supposition that his Lordship worked from an earlier manuscript than was furnished to Leigh Hunt for publication. Over and above the variations already given in foot-notes from the Houghton text (see Volume II, pages 357 to 360), the holograph shows the following. Stanza 3 originally stood thus—

> I see death's lilly on thy brow
>   With anguish moist and fever dew
> And on thy cheeks death's fading rose
>   Withereth too.

The word *death's*, however, is struck out in favour of *a* both in line 1 and in line 3; and *Fast* is put in before *withereth* in line 4. In Stanza 4, line 1 originally ended with *Wilds* (not *Wolds* as given by Mr. Colvin) instead of *Meads*. Line 2 of Stanza 7 originally stood thus—

> And honey wild and honey dew.

The only change made in the manuscript in this stanza is the substitution of *manna dew* for *honey dew*. There is no trace of the word *once* given by Mr. Colvin in *Macmillan's Magazine* in line 3. In the second line of Stanza 8 is the cancelled reading

> And there she wept and there she sigh'd . . .

and line 4 of Stanza 10 is

> Thee hath in thrall

instead of

> Hath thee in thrall!

Line 1 of Stanza 11 has the noun *gloam* which I felt tempted to retain in the text, as characteristic, on the suspicion that Hunt had substituted *gloom* in *The Indicator* without authority. Line 2 of the stanza had been begun with *All tremble* and had then been written

> With horrid warning wide agape

before the reading of the text was adopted; and finally there is a rejected opening of Stanza 12—

> And this is why I *wither*.—

It would be hard to find a single manuscript poem by Keats, of like extent, exceeding in interest that of *La Belle Dame sans Merci*; and the prose surroundings of the poem are no less interesting than the revisions of text shown in the draft of the poem itself. These surroundings will be found at large later on in the present volume, namely at pages 150 and 151; but I cannot refrain from a special reference in this place to the playful dissertation of the poet upon the number of kisses with which, in the early version, the "knight at arms" closed the eyes of the lady. The circumstance that Keats, fresh from the composition of this lovely poem, could find it in him to joke with his brother and sister-in-law about the lines

> And there I shut her wild wild eyes
> With kisses four

confirms me as to the train of thought which led to the rejection of that reading when the poem was published. If he could himself joke about the rejected version, he would naturally consider it open to jocular treatment by others; and that would be ample reason for finding another reading. But the important point in Keats's little joke against himself is that remarked on by Mr. Colvin (*Macmillan's Magazine*, August 1888), namely that it is "a proof the more of the spirit of humour, modesty, and plain sense which neither inspiration, nor the pride of inspiration, could conquer in him or long displace."

The last collation of which I have here to give the result is that of the noble Shakespearian fragment of *King Stephen* (Volume II, pages 475 to 485) with the manuscript in Lord Houghton's Keats collection. This manuscript consists of eight leaves—three quarto leaves in the writing of Charles Armitage Brown and five folio leaves in Keats's writing. Brown's first leaf has on the recto the title—

King Stephen.
a fragment
of a tragedy,
by
John Keats
Novr 1819—

while the verso bears the following list of

KING STEPHEN.

Dramatis Personæ.
King Stephen.
Duke of Glocester.
Earl of Chester.
Earl Baldwin.
The Empress Maud, or Matilda.

In Keats's text, however, Glocester is the Earl of Glocester. So far as Scene I is concerned, Brown's transcript corresponds with the published text save in line 35 (Volume II, page 476), where he reads *Not twenty Earl of Chesters,* instead of *Earls of Chester.* Brown's writing ends with *Now our dreaded Queen* (line 36) : Keats's begins with

enter another Captain
Glocester. What new . . .
What is't you would ~~speak~~ say ?

all of which is struck out for *Now our dreaded Queen*; so that those words stand repeated in the composite manuscript. The speech of the Second Captain (line 20) originally began with

This to thee
Most noble Gloster.

At the close of the speech, instead of *Enter Second Knight*, Keats wrote *Enter another Captain,* but struck the words out and substituted merely *a knight*; and for the rest of the scene the dialogue is between *Glocester* and *Knight* (not *Second Knight*). Line 36 originally began with *Maintains*, which was struck out for *Keeps elbow room.* Line 50 ends with *hilts*, not *hilt*; and I think Keats meant to use the plural. In line 51 Glocester says in the printed text, *Come, lead me to this man*: Keats certainly wrote *Lead me to this mars*; and doubtless he intended Glocester to compliment the fallen King by comparing him to the God of War, just as in the same scene Maud was compared to Pallas looking down from the walls of Ilion. It was nothing particular for Keats to spell a god's name with a small initial letter. Scene II is followed in Keats's manuscript by a cancelled opening of Scene III, thus—

Scene 3rd
The field of Battle—Enter Stephen unarm'd
Stephen Another Sword! for one short minute longer
That I may pepper that De Kaims and then
Yield to { ~~valliant~~ / ~~this army~~ } some twenty squadrons— { Stephen say / ~~This is glory!~~ }
Wouldst thou exchange this helmeted renown
To rule in qu[i]et Pylos Nestor-like?
No!——

Enter De Kaims Knights and Soldiers dropping in
De Kaims...

In rewriting the opening of the Scene, Keats at first put

Another Sword! and what if I took one
From forth Bellona's gleaming armoury

which stands altered to the far better reading of the text. Line 4 of the rewritten opening originally stood thus

Where is my Enemy? Aye, close at hand
Here comes the testy Brood

but this stands changed to the reading of the text, save

KING STEPHEN.

that *comes* is not altered to *come*. Line 15 stands thus—

  Yield Stephen, or my Sword's point ~~explore~~ dip in...

I scarcely think Keats meant this as an alternative present-future,

    or my sword's point dips in
  The gloomy current of a traitor's heart,

as Lord Houghton gave it: more probably he used *or* for *ere* or *before*. There is certainly no *s* either in *explore* or in *dip*. In line 27 *a king alive* is rejected for *a breathing king*; and before lines 30 and 31 were got to the poet's satisfaction he had gone through the following readings:

  To whi[s]per { there's the man who / there is he who } took alive
  King ...
  The stubborn Reb[el] ...

In line 44, again, occurs the plural *hilts*, not *hilt*, and in line 46 *Do ye hear!*—not *Do you hear?*

In line 10 of Scene IV *will I* stands for *I will*, and line 5 was written

  To sage advisers will I ever bend

but *will I* was struck out for *let me*. Line 13 was

  And not trench on our actions personal

but *not trenching* was substituted for *And not trench*. In line 32 *dreams sometimes* is rejected for *dreams too much*; and in the next line *out of date* is substituted for *weak enough*. Between lines 37 and 38 stands cancelled

  And finds for everyone of all his ...

The fragment ends with the words,

42 FRESH VERSES AND NEW READINGS.

<pre>   A Queen's nod
Can make ~~cold christmas~~ his June December—here he comes.
</pre>

The juxtaposition of Lord Houghton's *Lamia* and *King Stephen* manuscript fragments has caused me to observe the repetition of the notable phrase *sole and lone*: in *Lamia* we have

<pre>   A haunting music sole perhaps and lone
     Supportress of the faiery roof
</pre>

and in *King Stephen*

<pre>   He sole and lone maintains
     A hopeless bustle mid our swarming arms.
</pre>

From the appearance of this manuscript it would seem that, in November 1819, to throw off poetic utterances in the finest and freest style was as easy to Keats as the breathing of his native air.

The "Nonsense Verses" on Oxford which appear at page 74 of Volume IV, preserved by Charles Brown, but apart from any context, were also transcribed by Woodhouse, who connects them with an extract from a letter which Keats wrote to Reynolds from Oxford, and thus greatly increases their interest. It turns out that they are meant for a parody of a poem by Wordsworth. Keats seems to have written to Reynolds—

"Wordsworth sometimes, though in a fine way, gives us sentences in the style of school exercises.—For instance,

<pre>   The lake doth glitter,
          Small birds twitter &c.
</pre>

Now, I think this is an excellent method of giving a

very clear description of an interesting place such as Oxford is."

The particular poem of Wordsworth's thus alluded to was first published in 1807; and in Volume II (pages 9 and 10) of the collected Poems in two volumes which Wordsworth issued in 1815, it reappeared thus:

WRITTEN IN MARCH

While resting on the Bridge at the Foot of Brother's Water.

<pre>
    The cock is crowing,
    The stream is flowing,
    The small birds twitter,
    The lake doth glitter,
The green field sleeps in the sun;
    The oldest and youngest
    Are at work with the strongest;
    The cattle are grazing,
    Their heads never raising;
There are forty feeding like one!

    Like an army defeated
    The Snow hath retreated,
    And now doth fare ill
    On the top of the bare hill;
The Plough-boy is whooping—anon—anon;
    There's joy in the mountains;
    There's life in the fountains;
    Small clouds are sailing,
    Blue sky prevailing;
The rain is over and gone!
</pre>

Keats's criticism in this instance is better than his parody,—though the rhyme *common-hat* and *dominat*, bad enough in itself, has a certain aptness under the provocation of *fare ill* and *bare hill*. Woodhouse gives *Lives* instead of *Stands* as the first word of line 6, stanza 1; and he reads lines 2 and 3 of stanza 2 thus—

> O'er pale visages mourns
> The black tassel trencher, or common-hat.

The same authority gives the 16th of January 1818 as the date of the Sonnet to Mrs. Reynolds's Cat (Volume IV, pages 425-6), and does not credit Keats with misspelling *climacteric* and writing *has* for *hast* in line 1, or *has* for *have* in line 12. On the other hand he ends his transcript with *glass bottle wall*, while Hood gives the preferable reading *glass bottled wall.* In line 9 there is a genuine variation of epithet, *tender* for *dainty*.

The appreciation of Keats's genius which led so many of his intimates to preserve his most trifling effusions, and to transcribe them for each other even while he was yet alive, has thrown upon his editors of the present inquisitive and minutely studious age the not altogether grateful task of bringing into the tale of a great poet's works many trivialities and crudities that one would fain leave to oblivion if there were any option. These trifles, it is true, can never harm the poet's reputation, and are often in themselves amusing; but it is a pleasure to close the present sifting of new material with a sonnet[1] preserved by Woodhouse, not of Keats's, but by one

---

[1] Dated the 27th of February 1817, and already published by Mr. Colvin.

who was himself no mean poet, and who may fitly have the last word on an occasion like the present:

SONNET—TO KEATS

On reading his Sonnet written in Chaucer.

Thy thoughts, dear Keats, are like fresh-gathered leaves,
   Or white flowers pluck'd from some sweet lily bed;
   They set the heart a-breathing, and they shed
The glow of meadows, mornings, and spring eves,
Over the excited soul. Thy genius weaves
   Songs that shall make the age be nature-led,
   And win that coronal for thy young head
Which Time's strange hand of freshness ne'er bereaves.
Go on! and keep thee to thine own green way,
   Singing in that same key which Chaucer sung;—
Be thou companion of the Summer day,
   Roaming the fields, and olden woods among:—
So shall thy Muse be ever in her May;
   And thy luxuriant Spirit ever young.

J. H. Reynolds.

I shall be surprised if this sonnet does not find its way into future anthologies.

REVIEW OF JOHN HAMILTON REYNOLDS'S "PETER BELL, A LYRICAL BALLAD."

[The story of John Hamilton Reynolds's brilliant squib, *Peter Bell, a Lyrical Ballad*, is agreeably told by Keats at pages 145 and 149 of this volume; and the draft of the following review appears at pages 149 and 150. The review itself was published in *The Examiner* for Sunday the 25th of April 1819, and reappeared in the issue of Monday the 26th. Some of the variations from the draft seem to me to indicate that Keats himself made changes in copying it; but it is probable that Hunt is responsible for some of the alterations. Reynolds's *Peter Bell* (" the ante-natal Peter," as Shelley called it) is a scarce pamphlet, although there were three editions of it in a very short time. It is no longer out of currency; for it was reprinted, *totidem verbis*, as an appendix to the third volume of my library edition of Shelley's Poetical Works,— the volume containing *Peter Bell the Third*. In the genesis of that poem, it now appears, Keats took part; for it was this review, with Hunt's notice a week later of Wordsworth's *Peter Bell*, that so amused Shelley as to induce him to contribute to the *Bell* literature. The title-page of Reynolds's jeu d'esprit reads thus— " PETER BELL. A LYRICAL BALLAD. 'I do affirm that I am the REAL SIMON PURE.' *Bold Stroke for a Wife.* LONDON: PRINTED FOR TAYLOR AND HESSEY, 93, FLEET STREET. 1819." There is a page of advertisements at the end, wherein *Endymion* is offered for sale at 9s. This page is dated " April, 1819," in the first and second editions, and " May, 1819," in the third.—H. B. F.]

REVIEW OF JOHN HAMILTON REYNOLDS'S "PETER BELL, A LYRICAL BALLAD."

THERE have been lately advertised two books, both *Peter Bell* by name: what stuff one of them was made of may be seen by the motto,—" I am the real Simon Pure."—This false Florimel has hurried from the press, and obtruded herself into public notice, while, for ought we know, the real one may be still wandering about the woods and wildernesses. Let us hope she may soon appear, and make good her right to the Magic Girdle.

The pamphleteering Archimage, we can perceive, has rather a splenetic love, than a downright hatred, to real Florimels; he has, it seems, a fixed aversion to those three rising Graces, Alice Fell, Susan Gale, and Betty Foy; and now especially to Peter Bell, the fit Apollo.

It is plainly seen by one or two passages in this little skit, that the writer of it has felt the finer parts of Mr. WORDSWORTH'S poetry, and perhaps expatiated with his more remote and sublimer Muse. This, as far as it relates to *Peter Bell*, is unlucky: the more he may love the sad embroidery of the *Excursion*, the more will he hate the coarse sample[r]s of Betty Foy and Alice Fell; and, as they come from the same hand, the better will he be able to imitate that which we see can be imitated, to wit, *Peter Bell*, as far as that hero can be imagined from his obstinate name. We repeat, it is very unlucky: this Simon Pure is in points the very man: there is such a pernicious likeness in the scenery, such a pestilent humour in the rhymes, and such an inveterate cadence in some of the stanzas. If we are one part amused with this, we are three parts sorry that any one who has any appearance of appreciating WORDSWORTH, should show so much temper at this really provoking name of *Peter Bell*.

The following are specimens of the Preface and the Poetry:—

It is now a period of one-and-twenty years since I first wrote some of the most perfect compositions (except certain pieces I have written in my later days) that ever dropped from poetical pen. My heart hath been right and powerful all its years. I never thought an evil or a weak thought in my life. It has been my aim and my achievement to deduce moral thunder from buttercups, daisies *, celandines, and (as a poet, scarcely inferior to myself, hath it) "such small deer." Out of sparrows' eggs I have hatched great truths, and with sextons' barrows have I wheeled into human hearts, piles of the weightiest philosophy.

* * * * * * * * * *

My Ballads are the noblest pieces of verse in the whole range of English poetry: and I take this opportunity of telling the world I am a great man. Milton was also a great man. Ossian was a blind old fool. Copies of my previous works may be had in any numbers, by application at my publisher.

* * * * * *

> He hath a noticeable look †,
> This old man hath—this grey old man;
> He gazes at the graves, and seems,

---

* A favourite flower of mine. It was a favourite with Chaucer, but he did not understand its moral mystery as I do,

> "Little Cyclops, with one eye."
> *Poems by ME.*

† "A noticeable man with large grey eyes."
Lyrical Ballads.

With over waiting, over wan,
Like Susan Harvey's ‡ pan of creams.

'Tis Peter Bell—'tis Peter Bell,
Who never stirreth in the day;
His hand is wither'd—he is old!
On Sundays he is us'd to pray,
In winter he is very cold §.

I've seen him in the month of August,
At the wheat-field, hour by hour,
Picking ear,—by ear,—by ear,—
Through wind,—and rain,—and sun,—and shower,
From year,—to year,—to year,—to year.

You never saw a wiser man,
He knows his Numeration Table;
He counts the sheep of Harry Gill ‖,
Every night that he is able,
When the sheep are on the hill.

Betty Foy—*My* Betty Foy,
Is the aunt of Peter Bell;
And credit me, as I would have you,
Simon Lee was once his nephew,
And his niece is Alice Fell ‖ ‖.

He is rurally related;
Peter Bell hath country cousins,
(He had once a worthy mother)
Bells and Peters by the dozens,
But Peter Bell he hath no brother.

‡ Dairy-maid to Mr. Gill.
§ Peter Bell resembleth Harry Gill in this particular:

"His teeth they chatter, chatter, chatter."

I should have introduced this fact in the text, but that Harry Gill would not rhyme. I reserve this for my blank verse.

‖ Harry Gill was the original proprietor of Barbara Lewthwaite's pet-lamb; and he also bred Betty Foy's celebrated poney, got originally out of a Night-mare, by a descendant of the great Trojan horse.

‖ ‖ Mr. Sheridan, in his sweet poem of the Critic, supplies one of his heroes with as singularly clustering a relationship.

> Not a brother owneth he,
> Peter Bell he hath no brother;
> His mother hath no other son,
> No other son e'er call'd her mother;
> Peter Bell hath brother none.

The foregoing extracts were almost certainly not transcribed by Keats. They are so essentially accurate that they were in all probability set up from the pamphlet itself, or from portions of it cut out for the purpose. It is only in some half-a-dozen instances that it has been necessary to restore the punctuation of the original. The word *a* before *Night-mare*, four lines from the foot of the preceding page, seems to have been dropped out accidentally in *The Examiner*.

ON "RETRIBUTION, OR THE CHIEFTAIN'S DAUGHTER,"

A TRAGEDY

Acted at Covent Garden Theatre.

[This notice appeared in *The Champion* for Sunday the 4th of January 1818, under the editorship of John Scott. It is not nearly so good as the foregoing contribution to *The Examiner*, and does not seem to indicate that Keats would have been very successful if he had seriously attempted to trammel his genius by undertaking periodical hack work. For the circumstances in which this notice was written see page 76 of the present volume. The printing is very inexact ; and I have not thought it requisite to reproduce every trifling inaccuracy.—H. B. F.]

ON "RETRIBUTION, OR THE CHIEFTAIN'S DAUGHTER,"

A TRAGEDY

ACTED AT COVENT GARDEN THEATRE.

WHAT exquisite names did our old dramatists christen their plays withal! The title of an old play gives us a direct taste and surmise of its inwards, as the first lines of the Paradise Lost smack of the great Poem. The names of old plays are Dantean inscriptions over the gates of hell, heaven, or purgatory. Some of such enduring pathos that in these days we may not for decency utter them, 'honor dishonorable'—in these days we may but think of passion's seventh heaven, and but just mention how crystalline the third is. The old dramatists and their title pages are old Britain kings and their provinces. The fore page of a love play was ever "to Cupid's service bowed," as "The Mad Lover," "The Broken Heart"—or spake its neighbourhood to the "shores of old romance," as "The Winter's Tale," "The Two Noble Kinsmen."

The title of the play newly acted at Covent Garden set us thinking of these affairs. It had been long announced, and is called "Retribution, or the Chieftain's Daughter." Now this is most wretched; an unpardonable offence, so *sans pareilly*, so inferior to Mrs. Radcliffe, so germane to a play-bill at a fair, that we will say no

more about it for fear prejudice and indignation should carry us butt against the main body of the work, to try whose skull is hardest. The scene lies in Persia among "kingdoms of the sun." Varanes, king of Persia (Mr. Young), we learn, in conspiracy with his elder son Chofroo (Mr. Macready), had some time ago murdered his King and brother, for the sake of his Crown and Sceptre. It appears that Varanes tutored his son into the crime, and the son has the dreadful audacity to be continually holding a rod over his parent on account of the secret. This filial coercion as it touches upon Zimia the Chieftain's daughter (Miss O'Neill) begets the most leading features, and the greater number of speeches in the piece. Varanes has a younger son Hamed (Mr. C. Kemble), who is quite a contrast to Chofroo, being mild, gentle, and compassionate; and likewise most lionlike in his just wrath. These two contra-distinguished brothers are desperately in love with Zimia, whose father, Suthes (Mr. Terry), the tyrannical Chofroo had first driven into rebellion, by an improper behaviour to his daughter, afterwards conquered, and, sticking to the old proverb, talks of their being his slaves: he is opposed by Hamed—and thus one rut the carriage makes may be explored with all expostulations pro and con between the fathers, sons, and courtiers; moreover if the imaginer thinks in certain commonplaces about virtue and vice—virtue's footstool, and vice's ugly face, he will not be much out of the way. This Chofroo also has a great mind to displace his father by some means; however he is saved that trouble, for unluckily for Hamed during a perilous discourse between him and the King concerning the murder, the King is so overcome by "retribution" as to fall down in a fainting fit, not before his raving had called towards the room some gentlemen of the Court, who immediately apprehend Hamed for the murder of his father. In consequence Chofroo becomes sovereign, goes on in a most barefaced manner, and even when it is supposed his dead father is lying in state before him on his throne, he condemns Hamed, Suthes, and Zimia to death; they keep on moralizing and etiquetting upon who shall die, until in rushes Varanes, and turns the tables completely upon Chofroo who, instead of these innocents is led off to execution. There was a scene about a nosegay between Zimia, Hamed, and Suthes. We thought this most poetical part of the play, tedious, dull and bad. Some few expressions we caught at as poetical, such as in speaking of a waterfall, "cool enjoyment," with others of the like, could we recollect them. We have an idea too that the simile about autumn is fine. On the whole, however, it is full of improbabilities and common-place language, so that to refer it to any standard of excellence, it must be sear'd like—

> A scribbled form, drawn with a pen
> Upon a parchment.

In comparison with second rate, or rather no rate authors, we may say it is ten folios from Otway, and one-third as good as Rowe. If the author is young and has a wide chasm to fill up with achievement, and at the same time gives up writing such common-place as we find in this his first trial, he need not care what is said for or against in the public prints.

Miss O'Neill does a very fine thing about the third act, which cheers one up a little; we will not explain it, that those who go may also have the pleasure of surprise. Mr. C. Kemble kept us in very good temper. Mr. Young's acting we do not like, and therefore will not offend his numerous admirers with any remarks. Mr. Terry's talents have never been appreciated. Finally, we think the average excellence of the verse of this play, and the average excellence of the Covent Garden talent tragedian much upon a par, both for sentiment and pronunciation: more finally, that Miss O'Neill, and Mr. Kean are your only people to give music to the C. and S.

ON "DON GIOVANNI," A PANTOMIME
ACTED AT DRURY LANE THEATRE.

[The following notice, inferior, perhaps, even to that of *Retribution*, appeared in the same paper, namely *The Champion* for Sunday the 4th of January 1818. See pages 54 and 76 of this volume.—H. B. F.]

ON "DON GIOVANNI," A PANTOMIME

ACTED AT DRURY LANE THEATRE.

Don Giovanni after having been wire drawn for many years past at the neighbour theatres, made a pet of at the Surrey, and fiddled away to hell at the Italian Opera, has found its way into the Drury-lane pantomime for the Christmas of 1817-18. Your great antiquaries now would pronounce his whole history from the day of his birth to this present, not omitting the gradual changing of his hair from flaxen to black, nor any little choice conversation or riddle-me-ree between him and his nursery maid on the day he was breeched; nor how fond he was of rabbits, and pigeons, and cockchaffers, and moo-cows, and hunt the slipper, nor how he volunteered among the little tambour workers for weeks and weeks, so breathing in an intoxicating air, sucking in poison from a sampler, and forgetting himself at a red morocco slipper. Unfortunate Don! unthinkingly didst thou treasure up the forms of things in thine imagination—the storm, the fatal storm was mustering by little and little till it burst to the utter astonishment of a certain fair playmate. Then were his eyes opened, he forgot his kite, his top, and what is more his knitting needles—for now that happy time was gone where with a luxurious patience he would frame and fashion delicately a pair of garters for a being made of light. Aye happy and yet not happy was that May morning on which the young Giovanni and the fair Silentilla walked forth—but this is no place for a fairy tale; suffice it to say, that in consequence, has the poor youth been thrown into Tartarus from every stage in Europe, to the great delight of greater part of the male audience from a spirit of rivalry, jealousy, and certain other things which do haunt the heads and hearts of men, and to the retrospective compassion of the more soft and pitying spectators: he has, say they—

> ——— " Bought golden opinions—
> Which s[h]ould be worn now in their newest gloss,
> Not cast aside so soon."

In the course of the pantomime Punch and Judy with their family were introduced: an illustrious house, of which the pranks and witty squeaking are more popular than Giovanni himself; and it would not be an useless or uninstructive speculation to enquire why and wherefore. In the first place if the Don is well made, Punch is ill made; if the Rake has a dozen mistresses, Punch has his Judy, who has the charms of a dozen in her summed up—if the former has a confident stamp, the latter has the neatest jerk of the left leg; if the former has his quizzing glass the latter has his ladle. The Commentators have started a variety of frivolous objections to this entertaining hunchback; those of Stephanio one turns from disgusted, seeing that in his discourse concerning the wife Judy, he has punned upon the word *Lemon*. Malonius has objected to the bit of black ribbon which confines his pigtail, calling it an unapt contrast to the white powder, and saying moreover that it is a plagiarism from the chess board, the origin of which and that of the Punch family he thinks intimately connected. Theobaldio, Warburtonio, and many more make such like stands against all common sense and decency, with a blind sort of pertin[a]city, as if they were to seal the book of fame and remain unassailable by after critics. To answer these gentlemen separately would be to count the grains in a bushel of corn: to have a doubt of their vanity would be to take a hawk for a handsaw. One particular however may as well be noticed. Much cavilling has arisen concerning which of the ruined damsels shed the most tears, and to settle this matter we must turn, as naturally as horse to manger, towards tradition, from which we glean that three had black eyes, one blue, three hazel, six grey, and eight brown; is there any thing to be resolved on from this? One almost fears to say again we find from the secret memoirs of a lady-bird, the measurement the crique and breadth of their respective dimples: some ten, some twenty, some thirty paces across: yet this affords no clew to anything like probability. One of them, however, we learn, was in a few particulars distinct from the rest, and she we think must have been the most tearful unfortunate. Her finger nails were touched with the faintest crimson, like the heart of a maiden's blush; and if you did not suddenly snatch her into your vision, you might suppose that the fair roundure of her fingers reached back to heaven and faded into the milky way. She never plucked a lily but once.

As to the pantomime, be it good or bad, a child should write a critique upon it. We were pleased knowing how much better it ought to be—a child's is the eulogy—and that not merely in pantomimes.

FRESH LETTERS AND ADDITIONAL PASSAGES.

[By far the largest part of the following section is proper to the third volume of the Library edition. To avoid a wearisome repetition of the term "Volume III," the references are sometimes made to the relative page without repeating the mention of the volume. The reader should bear in mind, therefore, that the allusions to page so-and-so in the Italic portions of this section and in the foot-notes, up to page 156, are almost entirely to Volume III.—H. B. F.]

FRESH LETTERS AND ADDITIONAL PASSAGES.

[By far the largest part of the following section is proper to the third volume of the Library edition. To avoid a wearisome repetition of the term "Volume III," the references are sometimes made to the relative page without repeating the mention of the volume. The reader should bear in mind, therefore, that the allusions to page so-and-so in the Italic portions of this section and in the foot-notes, up to page 156, are almost entirely to Volume III.—H. B. F.]

FRESH LETTERS AND ADDITIONAL PASSAGES.

Since the publication of the library edition of Keats's Works in 1883, there has been an American issue of Lord Houghton's edition of the poetry, together with a volume of letters, superintended by Mr. J. G. Speed, who, being a grandson of George Keats, has had access to some of the papers formerly preserved at Louisville in Kentucky, and has been enabled to publish one new letter of considerable interest as well as to give several passages omitted from previous printed versions of Keats's letters. Later, Professor Sidney Colvin contributed to the "English Men of Letters" series an admirable volume on Keats, which, though based in the main upon previous publications, had the advantage of some fresh material. Notably Mr. Colvin had complete access to Lord Houghton's papers and to some manuscript books of Keats's friend Richard Woodhouse; and such writings of Keats as have been preserved in these records, but not used in Mr. Colvin's volume, he has kindly communicated to me,—allowing me also to use the autographs of Letters LVI, LXX, LXXXIV and LXXXVI, which have been placed in his care since his book came out. By means of the present Supplement I am adding to my edition all new material that is of consequence; and it is from the above-mentioned sources that the greater part of this material is drawn. *The significance of the new passages will be much enhanced by reading this section with Volumes III and IV at hand; and no difficulty will be found in connecting the compositions with the help of the indications given for that purpose in the ensuing pages.*

The following letter, which bears no post-mark, and was therefore probably sent by hand to Reynolds, appears to belong to the beginning of the year 1817, *and may be placed between No. IV and No. V in the third volume :—*

Sunday Evening

My dear Reynolds

Your kindness affects me so sensibly that I can merely put down a few mono-sentences—your criticism only makes me extremely anxious that I should not deceive you.

It's the finest thing by God—as Hazlitt would say. However I hope I may not deceive you.—There are some acquaintances of mine who will scratch their Beards and although I have, I hope, some Charity, I wish their nails may be long.—I will be ready at the time you mention in all Happiness.

There is a report that a young Lady of 16 has written the new Tragedy God bless her—I will know her by Hook or by Crook in less than a week—My Brother's and my Remembrances to your kind sisters.

yours most sincerely
John Keats

From the letter which Keats wrote to Reynolds when staying at Carisbrooke a passage has hitherto been omitted, at the commencement of the newly dated portion. Between " April 18*th* [1817]" *and* " *I'll tell you what," at page* 54 *of Volume III, insert :—*

Will you have the goodness to do this? Borrow a Botanical Dictionary—turn to the words Laurel and Prunes, show the explanations to your sisters and Mrs. Dilk[e] and without more ado let them send me the cups, Basket and Books they trifled and put off and off while I was in Town. Ask them what they can say for themselves—ask Mrs. Dilk[e] wherefore she does so distress me—let me know how Jane has her health—the weather is unfavourable for her.—Tell George and Tom to write.

The next new letter reads very much like the opening of the Oxford campaign. It is addressed to Miss Reynolds at Little Hampton, but is indicted to both Jane and Mariane Reynolds. Perhaps it will be safe to read it between No. XI (page 69) and No. XII (page 70) of the third volume; and No. XII has, it seems, been shorn of its first paragraph, which I now give at the close of this new letter for insertion before the words "Believe me".

Oxf—[ord, 5 Sept. 1817.]

My dear Friends,

You are I am glad to hear comfortable at Hampton, where I hope you will receive the Biscuits we ate the other night at Little Britain. I hope you found them good. There you are among Sands, stones, Pebbles, Beeches, Cliffs, Rocks, Deeps, Shallows, weeds, Ships Boats (at a distance) Carrots, Turnips, sun, moon, and stars and all those sort of things—here am I among Colleges, halls, Stalls, Plenty of Trees, thank God—Plenty of water, thank heaven—Plenty of Books, thank the Muses—Plenty of Snuff, thank Sir Walter Raleigh—Plenty of segars,—Ditto—Plenty of Flat country, thank

Tellus's rolling pin—I'm on the sofa—Buonaparte is on the snuff-box—But you are by the sea side—argal, you bathe—you walk—you say "how beautiful"—find out resemblances between waves and camels—rocks and dancing masters—fireshovels and telescopes—Dolphins and Madonas—which word, by the way, I must acquaint you was derived from the Syriac, and came down in a way which neither of you I am sorry to say are at all capable of comprehending—but as a time may come when by your occasional converse with me you may arrive at "something like prophetic Strain," I will unbar the gates of my pride and let my condescension stalk forth like a Ghost at the Circus—The word Ma-don-a, my dear Ladies—or—the word Mad-o-na—so I say! I am not mad.—Howsumever when that aged Tamer Kewthon sold a certain camel called Peter to the overseer of the Babel Sky works, he thus spake, adjusting his cravat round the tip of his chin—"My dear Ten-story-up-in-air! this here Beast, though I say it as shouldn't say't, not only has the power of subsisting 40 days and 40 nights without fire and candle but he can sing—Here I have in my Pocket a Certificate from Signor Nicolini of the King's Theatre; a Certificate to this effect . . . . . I have had dinner since I left that effect upon you, and feel too heavy in mentibus to display all the Profundity of the Polyglon—so you had better each of you take a glass of cherry Brandy, and drink to the health of Archimedes, who was of so benign a disposition that he never would leave Syracuse in his life—So kept himself out of all Knight Errantry—This I know to be a fact; for it is written in the 45th book of Winkine's treatise on garden-rollers, that he trod on a fishwoman's toe in Liverpool, and never begged her pardon. Now the long and short is this—that is by comparison—for a long day may be a short year—a long Pole may be a very stupid fellow as a man. But let us refresh ourself from this depth of thinking, and turn to some innocent jocularity—the Bow cannot always be bent—nor the gun always loaded, if you ever let it off —and the life of man is like a great Mountain—his breath is like a Shrewsbury cake—he comes into the world like a shoeblack, and goes out of it like a cob[b]ler—he eats like a chimney sweeper, drinks like a Gingerbread baker —and breathes like Achilles—so it being that we are such sublunary creatures, let us endeavour to correct all our bad spelling—all our most delightful abominations, and let us wish health to Marian and Jane, whoever they be and wherever—

your's truly
John Keats.

Oxford, Sunday Evening
[14 September 1817.]

My dear Jane

You are such a literal translator, that I shall some day amuse myself with looking over some foreign sentences, and imagining how you would render them into English. This is an age for typical curiosities; and I would advise you, as a good speculation, to study Hebrew, and astonish the world with a figurative version in our native tongue. The mountains skipping like rams, and the little hills like lambs, you will leave as far behind as the hare did the tortoise. It must be so or you would never have thought that I really meant you would like to pro and con about those honeycombs—no, I had no such idea; or, if I had, 'twould be only to teaze you a little for love. So now let us put down in black and white briefly my sentiments thereon. Imprimis I sincerely believe that Imogen is the finest creature, and that I should have been disappointed at hearing you prefer Juliet—Item—yet I feel such a yearning towards Juliet that I would rather follow her into Pandemonium than Imogen into Paradise—heartily wishing myself a Romeo to be worthy of her, and to hear the Devils quote the old proverb "Birds of a feather flock together." Amen.—Now let us turn to the sea-shore.

It may be mentioned that Woodhouse particularizes the date of this letter No. XII by the evidence of the post-mark, namely the 15*th of September* 1817. *The letter to Reynolds numbered XIII belongs to the* 21*st of September* 1817*; and the passage represented by the asterisks at the top of page* 75 *reads thus:*—"I think I see you and Hunt meeting in the Pit.—What a very pleasant fellow he is, if he would give up the sovereignty of a room pro bono —What evenings we might pass with him, could we have him from Mrs. H—Failings" &c. *The two blanks immediately afterwards should be filled up with the word* "*He*".

Letter No. XVI to Bailey (pages 82 *and* 83 *of the third volume) was given from Lord Houghton's version. As it consists, in that form, merely of some transposed and manipulated extracts, it is best to print it here in its integrity :—*

Hampstead, Octr Wednesday.
[8 October 1817.]

My dear Bailey,

After a tolerable journey I went from coach to Coach as far as Hampstead where I found my Brothers— the next Morning finding myself tolerably well I went to Lambs Conduit Street and delivered your parcel—Jane and Marianne were greatly improved, Marianne especially, she has no unhealthy plumpness in the face—but she comes me healthy and angular to the chin.—I did not see

John—I was extremely sorry to hear that poor Rice, after having had capital health—during his tour, was very ill. I dare say you have heard from him. From No. 19 I went to Hunt's and Haydon's who live now neighbours—Shelley was there—I know nothing about anything in this part of the world—everybody seems at Loggerheads. There's Hunt infatuated—there's Haydon's picture in statu quo—There's Hunt walks up and down his painting room—criticising every head most unmercifully. There's Horace Smith tired of Hunt. "The web of our life is of mingled yarn." Haydon having removed entirely from Marlborough Street—Crip[p]s must direct his letter to Lisson Grove, North Paddington. Yesterday morning while I was at Brown's, in came Reynolds, he was pretty bobbish, we had a pleasant day —he would walk home at night that cursed cold distance. Mrs. Bentley's children are making a horrid row—whereby I regret I cannot be transported to your Room to write to you—I am quite disgusted with literary men and will never know another except Wordsworth—no not even Byron. Here is an instance of the friendship of such, Haydon and Hunt have known each other many years—now they live—pour ainsi dire, jealous neighbours —Haydon says to me, Keats, don't show your lines to Hunt on any Account or he will have done half for you— so it appears Hunt wishes it to be thought. When he met Reynolds in the Theatre, John told him that I was getting on to the completion of 4000 lines—Ah ! says Hunt, had it not been for me they would have been 7000 ! If he will say this to Reynolds, what would he to other people ? Haydon received a Letter a little while back on this subject from some Lady—which contains a caution to me, thro' him, on the subject—now is not all this a most paultry thing to think about ? You may see the whole of the case by the following Extract from a Letter I wrote to George in the Spring—" As to what "you say about my being a Poet, I can return no answer "but by saying that the high idea I have of poetical "fame makes me think I see it towering too high above "me. At any rate, I have no right to talk until Endy- "mion is finished, it will be a test, a trial of my Powers "of Imagination, and chiefly of my invention which is a "rare thing indeed—by which I must make 4000 lines of "one bare circumstance, and fill them with poetry—and "when I consider that this is a great task, and that when "done it will take me but a dozen paces towards the "temple of fame—it makes me say—God forbid that I "should be without such a task! I have heard Hunt "say, and [I] may be asked—*why endeavour after a long* "*Poem?* To which I should answer. Do not the Lovers "of Poetry like to have a little Region to wander in, "where they may pick and choose, and in which the "images are so numerous that many are forgotten and "found new in a second Reading: which may be food "for a Week's stroll in the Summer? Do not they like "this better than what they can read through before Mrs "Williams comes down stairs? a morning work at most. "Besides, a long poem is a test of invention, which I take "to be the Polar Star of Poetry, as Fancy is the Sails— "and Imagination the rudder.—Did our great Poets ever "write Short Pieces? I mean in the shape of Tales— "This same invention seems indeed of late years to have "been forgotten as a Poetical excellence—But enough of "this, I put on no Laurels till I shall have finished "Endymion, and I hope Apollo is not angered at my "having made a Mockery at Hunts—"

You see Bailey how independent my Writing has been. Hunt's dissuasion was of no avail—I refused to visit

Shelley that I might have my own unfettered scope ;— and after all, I shall have the Reputation of Hunts elève. His corrections and amputations will by the knowing ones be traced in the Poem. This is, to be sure, the vexation of a day—nor would I say so many words about it to any but those whom I know to have my welfare and reputation at heart. Haydon promised to give directions for those casts, and you may expect to see them soon, with as many Letters—You will soon hear the dinning of Bells—never mind! you and Gle[i]g will defy the foul fiend—But do not sacrifice your health to Books : do take it kindly and not so voraciously. I am certain if you are your own Physician, your stomach will resume its proper strength and then what great benefits will follow.—My sister wrote a Letter to me, which I think must be at the post-office—Ax Will to see—My Brother's kindest remembrances to you—we are going to dine at Brown's where I have some hopes of meeting Reynolds. The little Mercury I have taken has corrected the poison and improved my health—tho' I feel from my employment that I shall never be again secure in Robustness. Would that you were as well as

     Your sincere friend and brother,
         John Keats.—

The letter which Lord Houghton described as the " Outside sheet of a letter to Mr. Bailey," and which occupies pages 84 and 85 of Volume III, is also incomplete, even as an outside sheet ; and it appears from the post-mark that the letter was sent on the 5th of November 1817. In place of the first line of asterisks, read as follows :—

I will speak of something else or my spleen will get higher and higher—and I am a bearer of the two-edged sword,—I hope you will receive an answer from Haydon soon, if not, Pride! Pride! Pride! I have received no more subscription—but shall soon have a full health, Liberty and leisure to give a good part of my time to him. I will certainly be in time for him—We have promised him one year: let that have elapsed, then do as we think proper. If I did not know how impossible it is, I should say—" do not at this time of disappointments, disturb yourself about others."—

I am now enabled to fill up the blanks in Letter No. XIX, pages 86 and 87. That in the second line of the text should contain the name of Cripps, the young man whom Haydon undertook to teach painting; and that in line 5 of page 87 should contain the name of Rice. Three lines further on, after the word " mother," occur the words " he was, soothly to sain." The asterisks at page 100 stand for very little: instead of " qualities " read " qualities, in sooth la!!"

The following letter, sent to George and Thomas Keats while they were in temporary residence at Teignmouth, should be read after letter No. XXII in the third volume, pages 98 to 100. I have collated Mr. Speed's version with the incomplete copy sent by Mr. Jeffrey to Lord Houghton:—

Featherstone Buildings, Monday.
[5 January 1818.]

My Dear Brothers:

I ought to have written before, and you should have had a long letter last week, but I undertook the "Champion" for Reynolds, who is at Exeter. I wrote two articles, one on the Drury Lane Pantomime, the other on the Covent Garden new Tragedy,[1] which they

---

[1] See Postscript. The tragedy was *Retribution, or the Chieftain's Daughter*,—the pantomime *Don Giovanni.* Keats's two papers

have not put in. The one they have inserted is so badly punctuated that, you perceive, I am determined never to write more without some care in that particular. Wells tells me that you are licking your chops, Tom, in expectation of my book coming out. I am sorry to say I have not begun my corrections yet: to-morrow I set out. I called on Sawrey this morning. He did not seem to be at all out at anything I said and the inquiries I made with regard to your spitting of blood, and moreover desired me to ask you to send him a correct account of all your sensations and symptoms concerning the palpitation and the spitting and the cough—if you have any. Your last letter gave me a great pleasure, for I think the invalid is in a better spirit there along the Edge[1]; and as for George, I must immediately, now I think of it, correct a little misconception of a part of my last letter. The Miss Reynolds have never said one word against me about you,[2] or by any means endeavoured to lessen you in my estimation. That is not what I referred to; but the manner and thoughts which I knew they internally had towards you, time will show. Wells and Severn dined with me yesterday. We had a very pleasant day. I pitched upon another bottle of claret. We enjoyed ourselves very much; were all very witty and full of rhyme. We played a concert[3] from 4 o'clock till 10—drank your healths, the Hunts', and *N. B.*

---

are reprinted in this volume from *The Champion* for 4 January 1818.

[1] It will be remembered that the brothers were on the sea coast.

[2] The curious locution may or may not be Keats's. What he meant, at all events, was to assure his brothers that the Misses Reynolds had not said anything *to* him *against* George.

[3] Each one, that is to say, imitated vocally some musical instru-

Severn, Peter Pindar's. I said on that day the only good thing I was ever guilty of. We were talking about Stephens[1] and the 1s. [?] Gallery. I said I wondered that careful folks would go there, for although it was but a shilling, still you had to pay through the Nose. I saw the Peachey family in a box at Drury one night. I have got such a curious,[2] or rather I had such, now I am in my own hand.

I have had a great deal of pleasant time with Rice lately, and am getting initiated into a little band. They call drinking deep dyin' scarlet. They call good wine a pretty tipple, and call getting a child knocking out an apple; stopping at a tavern they call hanging out. Where do you sup[3]? is where do you hang out?

Thursday I promised to dine with Wordsworth, and the weather is so bad that I am undecided, for he lives at Mortimer street. I had an invitation to meet him at Kingston's, but not liking that place I sent my excuse. What I think of doing to-day is to dine in Mortimer street (Wordsth), and sup here in the Feath^r buildings, as Mr. Wells[4] has invited me. On Saturday, I called on Wordsworth before he went to Kingston's, and was surprised to find him with a stiff collar. I saw his spouse, and I think his daughter. I forget whether I had written

---

ment, according to a custom in which Keats and his brothers and intimates indulged.

[1] Henry Stephens was one of Keats's fellow medical students.

[2] Mr. Speed notes that " a word is evidently omitted here."

[3] So according to Mr. Jeffrey and Mr. Speed; but *where do you stop* would be the proper equivalent nowadays, and would accord with the context.

[4] I suppose we may assume from this a single small fact in the occult biography of Charles Wells, to wit that in the winter of 1817-18 his people were living in Featherstone Buildings, a curious little court in Holborn.

my last before my Sunday evening at Haydon's—no, I did not, or I should have told you, Tom, of a young man you met at Paris, at Scott's, of the [name of] Ritchie.[1] I think he is going to Fezan, in Africa; then to proceed if possible like Mungo Park. He was very polite to me, and inquired very particularly after you. Then there was Wordsworth, Lamb, Monkhouse, Landseer, Kingston, and your humble servant. Lamb got tipsy and blew up Kingston—proceeding so far as to take the candle across the room, hold it to his face, and show us what a soft fellow he was.

I astonished Kingston at supper with a pertinacity in favour of drinking, keeping my two glasses at work in a knowing way.[2] He sent me a hare last week, which I sent to Mrs. Dilke. Brown is not come back. I and Dilke are getting capital friends. He is going to take the "Champion." He has sent his farce to Covent Garden. I met Bob Harris on the steps at Covent Garden; we had a good deal of curious chat. He came out with his old humble opinion. The Covent Garden pantomime is a very nice one, but they have a middling Harlequin, a bad Pantaloon, a worse Clown, and a shocking Columbine, who is one of the Miss Dennets.

I suppose you will see my critique on the new tragedy

---

[1] Joseph Ritchie, who started on his proposed journey, and died in Africa, wrote a charming poetical Farewell to England, which, as Mr. Garnett has pointed out to me, was printed by Alaric Watts in his *Poetical Album*. The reference to the house at which Tom Keats met Ritchie is extremely interesting, as indicating how poor John Scott probably became possessed of that copy-book of Tom's in which so many of the early poems of John Keats were written out fair by his younger brother.

[2] Although Lord Houghton does not give this letter, he mentions this particular incident.

in the next week's "Champion." It is a shocking bad one. I have not seen Hunt; he was out when I called. Mrs. Hunt looks as well as ever I saw her after her confinement. There is an article in the sennight "Examiner" on Godwin's "Mandeville," signed E. K. I think it Miss Kent's.[1] I will send it. There are fine subscriptions going on for Hone.

You ask me what degrees there are between Scott's novels and those of Smollet. They appear to me to be quite distinct in every particular, more especially in their aim. Scott endeavours to throw so interesting and romantic a colouring into common and low characters as to give them a touch of the sublime. Smollet, on the contrary, pulls down and levels what with other men would continue romance. The grand parts of Scott are within the reach of more minds than the finest humours in "Humphrey Clinker." I forget whether that fine thing of the Sargeant is Fielding's or Smollet's, but it gives me more pleasure than the whole novel of "The Antiquary." You must remember what I mean.[2] Some one says to the Sargeant: "That's a non-sequiter!" "If you come to that," replies the Sargeant, "you're another!"

I see by Wells' letter Mr. Abbey does not overstock you with money. You must write. I have not seen

---

[1] The article which Keats seems to have attributed to his admirer Miss Bessy Kent (Hunt's sister-in-law) was in fact by Shelley, "E. K." standing for "Elfin Knight," a pseudonym of Shelley's. The review appeared in *The Examiner* for Sunday the 28th of December 1817.

[2] "'Excuse me there, Mr. Serjeant,' quoth Partridge, 'that's a *non sequitur*.' 'None of your outlandish lingo,' answered the Serjeant, leaping from his seat; 'I will not sit and hear the cloth abused.'—'You mistake me, friend,' cries Partridge. 'I did not mean to abuse the cloth: I only said your conclusion was a *non sequitur*.' 'You are another,' cries the Serjeant, 'an' you come to

―¹ yet, but expect it on Wednesday. I am afraid it is gone. Severn tells me he has an order for some drawings for the Emperor of Russia.

I was at a dance at Redhall's, and passed a pleasant time enough—drank deep, and won 10£ at cutting for half crowns.² There was a younger brother of the ―― made himself very conspicuous after the ladies had retired from the supper table by giving mater [word illegible]. Mr. Redhall said he did not understand any thing but plain English, whereat Rice egged the young fool to say the word plainly out, after which there was an enquiry as to the derivation of the word ..... ―― said a very good thing, "Gentlemen," says he, "I have always understood it to be a root and not a derivative" .....

Bailey was there and seemed to enjoy the evening. Rice said he cared less about the hour than any one; and the proof is his dancing—he cares not for time, dancing as if he was deaf. Old Redhall not being used to give parties, had no idea of the quantity of wine that would be drank, and he actually put in readiness on the kitchen stairs eight dozen.

---

that, no more a sequitur than yourself.'"—Fielding's *Tom Jones*, Book IX, chapter 6.

¹ Mr. Speed says "The word is not legible, but he evidently referred to some play of the day." This is not at all evident to me.

² Mr. Jeffrey gives this passage as above; but Mr. Speed reads "10.6 at cutting for half guineas." No doubt the incident is the same as that referred to by Lord Houghton when he says Keats "speaks of having drunk too much as a rare piece of joviality, and of having won 10*l.* at cards as a great hit." Whether Mr. Speed or Mr. Jeffrey misread the letter who shall say? With reference to the gap in the letter Mr. Speed says, "In many places it is almost illegible ... and considering how many words I would have to leave to conjecture, I have concluded to omit the whole passage." Mr. Jeffrey attempted to copy it; but I have only been able to supply a portion from his imperfect transcript.

Every one inquires after you, and every one desires their remembrances to you. I have seen Fanny twice lately—she inquired particularly after you and wants a co-partnership letter from you. She has been unwell, but is improving—I think she will be quick well. Mrs. Abbey was saying that the Keatses were ever indolent, that they would ever be so, and that it is born in them. Well, whispered Fanny to me, if it is born with us, how can we help it. She seems very anxious for a letter. As I asked her what I should get for her, she said a "Medal of the Princess."[1] I called on Haslam—we dined very well. You must get well, Tom, and then I shall feel whole and genial as the winter air. Give me as many letters as you like, and write to Sawrey soon. I received a short letter from Bailey about Crip[p]s,[2] and one from Haydon, ditto. Haydon thinks he improved very much. Mrs. Wells' desires[3] particularly to Tom and her respects to George, and I desire no better than to be ever your most affectionate brother,

John.

P.S. I had not opened the "Champion" before. I found both my articles in it.

The next fresh letter which I have to give appears to have been written on the same morning as that to Haydon

---

[1] Of course a commemoration medal for the death of the Princess Charlotte, which had taken place the previous month, namely on the 6th of November 1817.

[2] See pages 80, 89, 96, 101, and 105 of Volume III.

[3] The expression "Mrs. Wells' desires," though quite an unusual one, may have been written by Keats and may possibly have been what he meant to write; but I do not remember meeting with this form of message elsewhere, either in Keats's letters or in those of any other writer.

numbered XXIII in Volume III. As to which of the two letters should come first, I find no evidence.

Saturday morning
[*Postmark*, 10 January 1818.]

My dear Taylor

Several things have kept me from you lately:—first you had got into a little hell, which I was not anxious to reconnoitre—secondly, I have made a vow not to call again without my first book: so you may expect to see me in four days. Thirdly, I have been racketing too much, and do not feel over well—I have seen Wordsworth frequently—Dined with him last Monday—Reynolds, I suppose you have seen—Just scribble me thus many lines to let me know you are in the land of the living, and well. Remember me to the Fleet Street Household—And should you see any from Percy Street, give my kindest regards to them.

your sincere friend John Keats

In Letter No. XXIV, at page 103, the following paragraphs should be inserted between the word "splendid" (line 6) and "I have just finished" (line 7):

I was speaking about doubts and fancies—I mean there has been a quarrel of a severe nature between Haydon and Reynolds and another ("the Devil rides upon a fiddle stick") between Hunt and Haydon. The first grew from the Sunday on which Haydon invited some friends to meet Wordsworth. Reynolds never went, and never sent any notice about it, this offended Haydon more than it ought to have done—he wrote a very sharp and high note to Reynolds and then another in palliation—but which Reynolds feels as an aggravation of the first.—Considering all things, Haydon's frequent neglect of his appointments &c., his notes were bad enough to put Reynolds on the right side of the question; but then Reynolds has no powers of sufferance; no idea of having the thing against him; so he answered Haydon in one of the most cutting letters I ever read; exposing to himself all his own weaknesses, and going on to an excess, which whether it is just or no, is what I would fain have unsaid, the fact is they are both in the right and both in the wrong.

The quarrel with Hunt I understand thus far. Mrs. H. was in the habit of borrowing silver of Haydon, the last time she did so, Haydon asked her to return it at a certain time—She did not—Haydon sent for it; Hunt went to expostulate on the indelicacy &c.—they got to words and parted for ever. All I hope is at some time to bring them all together again.—Lawk! Molly there's been such doings—Yesterday evening I made an appointment with Wells to go to a private theatre, and it being in the neighbourhood of Drury Lane and thinking we might be fatigued with sitting the whole evening in one dirty hole; I got the Drury Lane ticket and therewith we divided the evening with a spice of Richard III.—

Good Lord! I began this letter nearly a week ago, what have I been doing since—I have been—I mean not been sending last Sunday's paper to you I believe because it was not near me—for I cannot find it and my conscience presses heavy on me for not sending it; you would have had one last Thursday, but I was called away, and have been about somewhere ever since. Where? What? Well I rejoice almost that I have not heard from you, because no news is good news. I cannot for the world recollect why I was called away; all I know is, that there has been a dance at Dilke's and another at the London Coffee House; to both of which

I went. But I must tell you in another letter the circumstances thereof—for though a week should have passed since I wrote on the other side it quite appals me—I can only write in scraps and patches. Brown is returned from Hampstead—Haydon has returned an answer in the same style—they are all dreadfully irritated against each other—On Sunday I saw Hunt and dined with Haydon, met Hazlitt and Bewick there; and took Haslam with me—forgot to speak about Crip[p]s though I broke my engagement to Haslam's on purpose—Mem. Haslam came to meet me, found me at breakfast, had the goodness to go with me my way.

In Letter XXV as printed by Lord Houghton, Keats's extract from Haydon's letter has been retrenched. The asterisks should be replaced by this not very mellifluous passage:

Thus I will do, and this will be effectual, and as I have not done it for any other human being, it will have an effect.

The letter has also a postscript—

If Reynolds calls tell him three lines will be acceptable, for I am squat at Hampstead.

From Letter No. XXVII to George and Thomas Keats, Lord Houghton's omissions were considerable. After the enumeration of friends whom Keats met at Hazlitt's lecture should come the following passage, between "aye and more" and "I think" (page 108) :

The Landseers enquired after you particularly—I know not whether Wordsworth has left town—But sunday I dined with Hazlitt and Haydon, also that I took Haslam with me—I dined with Brown lately. Dilke having taken the Champion Theatricals was obliged to be in town. Fanny has returned to Walthamstow. Mr. Abbey appeared very glum the last time I went to see her, and said in an indirect way, I had no business to be there. Rice has been ill, but has been mending much lately.

The asterisks at page 109 should be replaced by the following passage:

I left off short in my last just as, I began an account of a private theatrical—Well it was of the lowest order, all greasy and oily, insomuch that if they had lived in olden times, when signs were hung over the doors; the only appropriate one for that oily place would have been—a guttered candle.—They played John Bull, The Review, and it was to conclude with Bombastes Furioso— I saw from a Box the 1st Act of John Bull, then went to Drury and did not return till it was over; when by Wells' interest we got behind the scenes—there was not a yard wide all the way round for actors, scene shifters and interlopers to move in; for 'Nota Bene' the Green Room was under the stage, and there was I threatened over and over again to be turned out by the oily scene shifters. There did I hear a little painted Trollop own, very candidly, that she had failed in Mary, with a "damned if she'd play a serious part again, as long as she lived," and at the same time she was habited as the Quaker in the Review—there was a quarrel and a fat good natured looking girl in soldiers clothes wished she had only been a man for Tom's sake,—One fellow began a song but an unlucky finger-point from the Gallery sent him off like a shot. One chap was dressed to kill for the King in Bombastes, and he stood at the edge of the scene in the very sweat of anxiety to show himself, but alas the thing was not played. The sweetest morsel of the night moreover was, that the musicians began pegging and fagging away—at an overture—never did you see faces more in earnest, three times did they play it over, dropping all kinds of correctness and still did not the curtain go up. Well then they went into a country-dance, then into a region they well knew, into the old boonsome Pothouse, and then to see how pompous o' the sudden they turned; how they looked about and chatted; how they did not care a damn; was a great treat—I hope I have not tired you by this filling up of the dash in my last.

From Letter XXIX, again, Lord Houghton omitted the opening. Instead of the asterisks, should stand at page 111, *the following paragraph:*

My dear Reynolds

I have parcell'd out this day for Letter Writing—more resolved thereon because your Letter will come as a refreshment and will have (sic parvis &c) the same effect as a kiss in certain situations where people become overgenerous. I have read this first sentence over, and think it savours rather; however an inward innocence is like a nested dove; or as the old song says—

O blush not so, O blush not so, &c.[1]

Between the words " simplicity is the only thing" and " It may be said," in the letter to Reynolds numbered XXX, page 112 *of Volume III, should be inserted—*

The first is the best on account of the first line, and

---

[1] Here follows the whole song which is printed at pages 279 and 280 of Volume II, under the title of *Sharing Eve's Apple.*

the "arrow foil'd of its antler'd food"—and moreover (and this is the only word or two I find fault with, the more because I have had so much reason to shun it as a quicksand) the last has "tender and true". We must cut this, and not be rattlesnaked into any more of the like.

After quoting the Lines on the Mermaid Tavern in the same letter, Keats seems to have written thus (page 114):—

I will call on you at 4 tomorrow and we will trudge together for it is not the thing to be a stranger in the Land of Harpsicols. I hope also to bring you my 2^d Book.

The next fresh letter which I have to insert should be read between those numbered XXX and XXXI, pages 114 and 115 of the third volume. It refers to "Endymion."

Fleet St. Thursd: Morn.
[5 February 1818.]

My dear Taylor,

I have finished copying my 2^d Book—but I want it for one day to overlook it—And moreover this day I have very particular employ in the affair of Cripps—so I trespass on your indulgence, and take advantage of your goodnature. You shall hear from me or see me soon. I will tell Reynolds of your engagement tomorrow.

yrs unfeigned^{ly},
John Keats.

Letter XXXI to George and Thomas Keats, as given at pages 115 and 116 of Volume III, was shorn by Lord Houghton of two short passages: between "copied it all" and "Hazlitt's last lecture" (page 115) we should read—

Horace Smith has lent me his manuscript called "Nehemiah Muggs, an exposure of the Methodists"—perhaps I may send you a few extracts.

And at the end, after "Popular Preachers," should stand the words—

All the talk here is about Dr. Croft, the Duke of Devon etc.

The next letter to his brothers, numbered XXXIII, also requires completion. In the first paragraph (page 120), between the words "Horace Smith" and "I received", should stand—

The occasion of my writing to-day is the enclosed letter, by Postmark, from Miss W—— Does she expect you in town George?

And after "Uriel", at the end of the paragraph, should be this additional one:

Reynolds has been very ill for some time confined to the house, and had leeches applied to the chest; when I saw him on Wednesday he was much the same, and he is in the worst place for amendment, among the strife [of] women's tongues, in a hot parch'd room: I wish he would move to Butler's for a short time.

At page 121, line 2, instead of "they are kind to me," we should read "we are very thick; they are very kind to me, they are well"; and the asterisks after the word "readiness" stand in place of an interesting allusion to a contemporary poet of the first magnitude:

I am sorry that Wordsworth has left a bad impression wherever he visited in town by his egotism, vanity and bigotry, yet he is a great poet if not a philosopher.

In Letter XXXIV, to Taylor, the references to "Endymion" when given in full, instead of in the truncated form in which they appear in the fourth paragraph (page 123), stand thus:

I have copied the Third Book and begun the Fourth. On running my eye over the proofs, I saw one mistake—I will notice it presently, and also any others, if there be any. There should be no comma in "the raft branch down sweeping from a tall ash-top." I have besides made one or two alterations and also altered the 13th line p. 32 to make sense of it, as you will see. I will take care the printer shall not trip up my heels. There should be no dash after Dryope, in the line "Dryope's lone lulling of her child."

From Letter XL, to James Rice, a passage of much humour was excised by Lord Houghton. It should be between the words " sow-sow-west " and the allusion to Dawlish fair, at page 137.

Some of the little Bar-maids look'd at me as if I knew Jas. Rice—but when I took (cherry ?) Brandy they were quite convinced. One asked whether you (preserv ?)-ed a secret she gave you on the nail—Another, how many buttons of your coat were buttoned in general.—I told her it used to be four—But since you had become acquainted with one Martin you had reduced it to three, and had been turning this third one in your mind—and would do so with finger and thumb only you had taken to snuff. I have met with a brace or twain of little Long-heads—not a bit o' the German. All in the neatest little dresses, and avoiding all the puddles, but very fond of peppermint drops, laming ducks and . . . . Well, I can't tell! I hope you are shewing poor Reynolds the way to get well.

The asterisks at page 146 (Letter XLIV, to Reynolds) stand for something more than the stanzas which Keats copied from "Isabella" for his friend's edification. These appear to have been followed by the words—

I heard from Rice this morning—very witty—and have just written to Bailey—Don't you think I am brushing up in the letter way? and being in for it you shall hear again from me very shortly:—if you will promise not to put hand to paper for me until you can do it with a tolerable ease of health—except it be a line or two.

Again from Letter XLV a paragraph was omitted by Lord Houghton, and should follow the first paragraph (page 147):

I think those speeches which are related—those parts where the Speaker repeats a speech, such as Glaucus's repetition of Circe's words, should have inverted commas to every line. In this there is a little confusion. If we divide the speeches into identical and related; to the former put merely one inverted comma at the beginning and another at the end; to the latter inverted commas before every line, the book will be better understood at the first glance—Look at pages 126, 127, you will find in the 3^d line the begin[n]ing of a related speech marked thus " Ah! art awake—" while, at the same time, in the next page the continuation of the *identical* speech is marked in the same manner " young man of Latmos "— you will find on the other side all the parts which should have inverted commas to every line.

At page 149, between the quotation from Milton and the statement that Tom wants to be in town, should appear the curious sentence " I shall breathe worsted stockings sooner than I thought for." *And, continuing the same letter to Reynolds, we come to an omission at page* 153. *The asterisks should be replaced by this passage :—*

Have you not seen a gull, an orc, a sea-mew, or anything to bring this Line to a proper length, and also fill up this clear part ; that like the gull I may *dip*—I hope, not out of sight—and also, like a gull, I hope to be lucky in a good sized fish.

Woodhouse has recorded that the first page of the letter was crossed, and that the first two lines, being written in the margin, stood out clearly, while the word " dip " was the first word that dipped into the obscurity of the writing which at that point Keats began to cross.

Between Letters XLVIII and XLIX may be read the following fresh one.

Sunday evening,
[21 June 1818.]

My dear Taylor,

I am sorry I have not had time to call and wish you health till my return. Really I have been hard run these last three days. However, au revoir, God keep us all well! I start tomorrow Morning. My brother Tom will I am afraid be lonely. I can scarcely ask the loan of books for him, since I still keep those you lent me a year ago. If I am overweening, you will I know be indulgent. Therefore when you shall write, do send him some you think will be most amusing—he will be careful in returning them. Let him have one of my books bound. I am ashamed to catalogue these messages. There is but one more, which ought to go for nothing as there is a lady concerned. I promised Mrs.

Reynolds one of my books bound. As I cannot write in it let the opposite be pasted in 'prythee. Remember me to Percy St.—Tell Hilton that one gratification on my return will be to find him engaged on a history piece to his own content. And tell Dewint I shall become a disputant on the landscape. Bow for me very genteely to Mrs. D. or she will not admit your diploma. Remember me to Hessey, saying I hope he'll *Carey* his point. I would not forget Woodhouse. Adieu!

Your sincere friend,

John o'Grots.

In Letter XLIX after "Helm Crag" (page 164, line 20) should be the words—" We shall proceed immediately to Carlisle, intending to enter Scotland on the 1st of July viâ ———." *In Letter LI, the passage about the kirk (at page 171) should stand thus after the words " Scotch Kirk" in line* 14—"A Scotch girl stands in terrible aw[e] of the Elders—poor little Susannahs. They will scarcely laugh; and their Kirk is greatly to be damned. These Kirk-men have done Scotland good (Query?)." *Then should come " They have made men", &c., as at page* 171, *down to "neighbourhood" in line* 21. *Then between that and " How sad" in line* 24, *should stand instead of the words printed by Lord Houghton and followed in my edition:—* "These Kirk-men have done Scotland harm; they have banished puns, and laughing and kissing &c. (except in cases where the very danger and crime must make it very gustful). I shall make a full stop at kissing, for after that there should be a better parenthesis, and go on to remind you of the fate of Burns:—poor, unfortunate fellow! his disposition was Southern!"

Letter LII, to Reynolds, needs to be completed by the

insertion of the following additional paragraph between the last and the last but one (page 179):

The short stay we made in Ireland has left few remembrances—but an old woman[1] in a dog-kennel Sedan with a pipe in her Mouth, is what I can never forget—I wish I may be able to give you an idea of her—Remember me to your Mother and Sisters, and tell your Mother how I hope she will pardon me for having a scrap of paper pasted in the Book sent to her.[2] I was driven on all sides and had not time to call on Taylor.—So Bailey is coming to Cumberland—well, if you'll let me know where at Inverness, I will call on my return and pass a little time with him—I am glad 'tis not Scotland.

Letter LVI as printed at pages 198 *to* 203 *of the third volume shows a few verbal variations from the holograph, has been a little rearranged towards the close, and lacks the following passages:*

Have you heard in any way of George? I should think by this time he must have landed—I in my carelessness never thought of knowing where a letter would find him on the other side—I think Baltimore but I am afraid of directing it to the wrong place. I shall begin some chequer work for him directly and it will be ripe for the post by the time I hear from you next after this. . . . With respect to women I think I shall be able to conquer my passions hereafter better than I have yet

---

[1] The old woman was of course the same whom Keats has immortalized by his inimitable portrait of "the Duchess of Dunghill," in his letter to Tom begun at Auchencairn (pages 173-4).

[2] Woodhouse explains that Keats wrote "from the Author" on a scrap of paper which he left to be pasted into a copy of *Endymion* when sent to Mrs. Reynolds. See top of preceding page.

done. You will help me to talk of George next winter and we will go now and then to see Fanny. Let me hear a good account of your health and comfort telling me truly how you do alone.

In the letter to Mrs. Wylie, page 212 of Volume III, line 14, Keats appears to have perpetrated the mild joke of writing " werry" (underlined) instead of " very." After the words " smoking on a large scale," Mr. Jeffrey's transcript gives another sentence—

Besides riding about 400, we have walked about 600 miles, and may therefore reckon ourselves as set out.

According to the same authority, the final paragraph begins with " I wish, my dear Madam," instead of " I assure you, my dear Madam."

The letter to Benjamin Bailey numbered LXII in this edition and printed at pages 218 to 222 of the third volume, I gave with the place and date assigned to it by Lord Houghton, " Teignmouth, September 1818," expressing, however, some doubt as to the correctness of the date. Mr. Colvin shows that the true date is Friday the 13th of March 1818; and thus the supposition that Keats and his brother Tom made two journeys to Teignmouth in 1818, one in the spring and one in the autumn, falls to the ground. Mr. Colvin traces the mistake in the date back to Woodhouse,—whose exactness in such matters might well impose upon Lord Houghton. My reasons for doubting his Lordship's date are adduced by Mr. Colvin as proof of its incorrectness: proof they certainly are not; and they did not justify me in classing the letter with those of the spring. The real proof appears to have been found by Mr. Colvin among Lord Houghton's papers, which I was unable to examine, though invited to do so at Fryston Hall.

This letter No. LXII should in future, I think, stand between No. XXXV and No. XXXVI.

Letter LXX (pages 235 to 245 of Volume III) has been a good deal cut down and manipulated: many of the verbal changes, though impertinent and meaningless, are of minor consequence; but there are passages which I must now take the opportunity of restoring from the holograph. After the word " acquainted", four lines from the foot of the text at page 235, should be inserted—

This sentence should it give you any uneasiness do not let it last for before I finish it will be explained away to your satisfaction.

And in place of " Your welfare is a delight to me which I cannot express," at the opening of the new paragraph on page 236, should be the corresponding passage—

I will relieve you of one uneasiness overleaf. I returned I said on account of my health—I am now well from a bad sore throat which came of bog trotting in the Island of Mull—of which you shall hear by the copies I shall make from my Scotch Letters. Your content in each other is a delight to me which I cannot express.

Instead of the short paragraph forming lines 6 to 12 of page 237, we should read as follows:

Tomorrow I shall call on your Mother and exchange information with her. On Tom's account I have not been able to pass so much time with her as I would otherwise have done. I have seen her but twice—one I dined with her and Charles. She was well, in good spirits and I kept her laughing at my bad jokes. We went to tea at Mrs. Millar's and in going were particularly struck with the light and shade through the Gateway at the Horse Guards. I intend to write you such volumes that it will be impossible for me to keep any order or method in what I write: that will come first which is uppermost in my mind, not that which is uppermost in my heart—besides I should wish to give you a picture of our Lives here whenever by a touch I can do it; even as you must see by the last sentence our walk past Whitehall all in good health and spirits—this I am certain of, because I felt so much pleasure from the simple idea of your playing a game of Cricket. At Mrs. Millar's I saw Henry quite well—there was Miss Keasle—and the goodnatured Miss Waldegrave—Mrs. Millar began a long story and you know it is her Daughter's way to help her on as though her tongue were ill of the gout. Mrs. M. certainly tells a story as though she had been taught her alphabet in Crutched Friars. Dilke has been very unwell; I found him very ailing on my return—he was under Medical care for some time, and then went to the sea side whence he has returned well. Poor little Mrs. D. has had another gall-stone attack; she was well ere I returned—she is now at Brighton. Dilke was greatly pleased to hear from you and will write a letter for me to enclose—He seems greatly desirous of hearing from you of the settlement itself—

Between the allusions to horn spoons and Reynolds's return from Devonshire, at page 237, stands this sentence:

Severn has had a narrow escape of his Life from a Typhous fever: he is now gaining strength.

And between the two paragraphs at page 238 there is another omitted passage:

Poor Haydon's eyes will not suffer him to proceed with his picture—he has been in the Country.—I have seen him but once since my return. I hurry matters together here because I do not know when the Mail sails —I shall enquire tomorrow and then shall know whether to be particular or general in my letter—you shall have at least two sheets a day till it does sail whether it be three days or a fortnight—and then I will begin a fresh one for the next Month.

At the close of the celebrated passage about Miss Jane Cox ("Charmian"), immediately before the quotation from Byron (page 240) should stand the words—"Do not think my dear Brother from this that my Passions are headlong or likely to be ever of any pain to you"—and after the words "I have no town talk for you" Keats wrote "as I have not been much among people." Near the beginning of the next page stands a vile expression which is not Keats's—"because of the sake of éclat": the holograph reads "for the sake of éclat," and eight lines lower on the same page Keats's expression was "We breathe in a sort of Officinal admosphere." The poem "A Prophecy," mentioned in the foot-note at page 242, is followed by a long omitted passage, namely:

This is friday, I know not what day of the Month—I will enquire tomorrow for it is fit you should know the time I am writing. I went to Town yesterday and calling at Mrs. Millar's was told that your Mother would not be found at home—I met Henry as I turned the corner—I had no leisure to return, so I left the letters with him. He was looking very well. Poor Tom is no better to-night—I am afraid to ask him what Message I shall send for him. And here I could go on complaining of my Misery, but I will keep myself cheerful for your sakes. With a great deal of trouble I have succeeded in getting Fanny to Hampstead. She has been several times. Mr. Lewis has been very kind to Tom all the summer there has scarce a day passed but he has visited him and not one day without bringing or sending some fruit of the nicest kind. He has been very assiduous in his enquiries after you. It would give the old Gentleman a great deal of pleasure if you would send him a sheet enclqsed in the next parcel to me, after you receive this—how long it will be first.—Why did I not write to Philadelphia? Really I am sorry for that neglect. I wish to go on writing ad infinitum to you—I wish for interesting matter and a pen as swift as the wind. But the fact is I go so little into the Crowd now that I have nothing fresh and fresh every day to speculate upon except my own whims and theories. I have been but once to Haydon's, once to Hunt's, once to Rice's, once to Hessey's. I have not seen Taylor, I have not been to the Theatre. Now if I had been many times to all these I could on my return at night have each day something new to tell you of without any stop. But now I have such a dearth that when I get to the end of this sentence and to the bottom of this page I much [*sic*] wait till I can find something interesting to you before I begin another. After all it is not much matter what it may be about, for the very words from such a distance penned by this hand will be grateful to you— even though I were to copy out the tale of Mother Hubbard or Little Red Riding Hood. I have been over to Dilke's this evening—there with Brown we have been talking of different and indifferent Matters—of Euclid, of Metaphisics, of the Bible, of Shakespeare, of the horrid system and conseque[nce]s of the fagging at great schools. I know not yet how large a parcel I can send—I mean by way of Letters—I hope there can be no objection to my dowling up a quire made into a small compass. That is the manner in which I shall write. I shall send you more than Letters—I mean a tale which I must begin on account of the activity of my Mind; of its inability to remain at rest. It must be prose and not very exciting. I must do this because in the way I am at present situated I have too many interruptions to a train of feeling to be able to write Poetry. So I shall write this Tale, and if I think it worth while get a duplicate made before I send it off to you.

This is a fresh beginning the 21st October. Charles and Henry were with us on Sunday and they brought me your Letter to your Mother—we agreed to get a Packet off to you as soon as possible. I shall dine with your Mother tomorrow when they have promised to have their Letters ready. I shall send as soon as possible without thinking of the little you may have from me in the first parcel, as I intend as I said before to begin another Letter of more regular information. Here I want to communicate so largely in a little time that I am puzzled where to direct my attention. Haslam has promised to let me know from Capper and Hazlewood. For want of something better I shall proceed to give you some extracts from my Scotch Letters. But now I think on it why not send you the letters themselves—I have three of them at present, I believe Haydon has two which I will get in time. I dined with your Mother and Henry at Mrs. Millar's on Thursday when they gave me their Letters—Charles' I have not yet—he has promised to send it. The thought of sending my Scotch Letters has determined me to enclose a few more which I have received and which will give you the best cue to how I am going on better than you could otherwise know. Your Mother was well and I was sorry I could not stop later. I called on Hunt yesterday—it has been always my fate to meet Ollier there. On Thursday I

walked with Hazlitt as far as covent Garden: he was
going to play Rackets. I think Tom has been rather
better these few last days—he has been less nervous. I
expect Reynolds tomorrow. Since I wrote thus far I
have met with that same Lady again, whom I saw at
Hastings and whom I met when we were going to the
English Opera. It was in a street which goes from
Bedford Row to Lamb's Conduit Street. I passed her
and turned back: she seemed glad of it; glad to see me
and not offended at my passing her before. We walked
on towards Islington where we called on a friend of her's
who keeps a Boarding School. She has always been an
enigma to me—she has been in a Room with you and
Reynolds and wishes we should be acquainted without
any of our common acquaintance knowing it. As we
went along, sometimes through shabby, sometimes
through decent Streets I had my guessing at work not
knowing what it would be and prepared to meet any
surprise. First it ended at this House at Islington: on
parting from which I pressed to attend her home. She
consented and then again my thoughts were at work
what it might lead to, tho' now they had received a sort
of genteel hint from the Boarding School. Our Walk
ended in 34 Gloucester Street Queen Square—not
exactly so for we went up stairs into her sitting room, a
very tasty sort of place with Books, Pictures, a bronze
statue of Buonaparte, Music, aeolian Harp; a Parrot, a
Linnet. A case of choice Lique[u]rs &c. &c. She behaved
in the kindest manner—made me take home a Grouse
for Tom's dinner. Asked for my address for the pur-
pose of sending more game. As I had warmed with her
before and kissed her I thought it would be living back-
wards not to do so again—she had a better taste: she
perceived how much a thing of course it was and shrunk

from it—not in a prudish way but in as I say a good taste. She continued to disappoint me in a way which made me feel more pleasure than a simple kiss could do. She said I should please her much more if I would only press her hand and go away. Whether she was in a different disposition when I saw her before—or whether I have in fancy wrong'd her I cannot tell. I expect to pass some pleasant hours·with her now and then: in which I feel I shall be of service to her in matters of knowledge and taste: if I can I will. I have no libidinous thought about her—she and your George are the only women à peu près de mon age whom I would be content to know for their mind and friendship alone. I shall in a short time write you as far as I know how I intend to pass my life—I cannot think of those things now Tom is so unwell and weak.

Again at the close of this important letter much has been left out: instead of the brief passage from " Tom is rather more easy" (page 244) to the close, the holograph reads thus:

Haslam has been here this morning and has taken all the Letters except this sheet, which I shall send him by the Twopenny, as he will put the Parcel in the Boston post Bag by the advice of Capper and Hazlewood, who assure him of the safety and expedition that way—the Parcel will be forwarded to Warder and thence to you all the same. There will not be a Philadelphia ship for these six weeks—by that time I shall have another Letter to you. Mind you I mark this letter A. By the time you will receive this you will have I trust passed through the greatest of your fatigues. As it was with your Sea sickness I shall not hear of them till they are past. Do not set to your occupation with too great an anxiety—take it calmly—and let your health be the

prime consideration. I hope you will have a son, and it is one of my first wishes to have him in my Arms—which I will do please God before he cuts one double tooth. Tom is rather more easy than he has been: but is still so nervous that I cannot speak to him of these Matters —indeed it is the care I have had to keep his Mind aloof from feelings too acute that has made this Letter so short a one—I did not like to write before him a Letter he knew was to reach your hands. I cannot even now ask him for any Message—his heart speaks to you. Be as happy as you can. Think of me and for my sake be cheerful.
        Believe me my dear Brother and Sister
        Your anxious and affectionate Brother
                John

This day is my birthday—
All our friends have been anxious in their enquiries and all send their remembrances.

Between Letters LXXVI and LXXVII (pages 252 and 253) may be read the following new one.

        Wentworth Place [24 Dec. 1818.]
My dear Taylor
    Can you lend me £30 for a short time? ten I want for myself—and twenty for a friend—which will be repaid me by the middle of next month. I shall go to Chichester on Wednesday and perhaps stay a fortnight—I am afraid I shall not be able to dine with you before I return—
Remember me to Woodhouse
            Yours sincerely
                John Keats

Of the long and important letter of 1818-19, *No. LXXXIV, to George and Georgiana Keats, the holograph is fortunately extant and accessible, although Mr. Speed does not seem to have seen it. Among the many unwarrantable interferences with the text, to which Keats's letters have been subjected, few exceed in calm misrepresentation the closing sentence of the first paragraph (page 264 of the third volume) as hitherto printed. Instead of the words "I have a firm belief in immortality, and so had Tom," the holograph contains this passage:—*

I have scarce a doubt of immortality of some nature of [sic] other—neither had Tom. My friends have been exceedingly kind to me every one of them—Brown detained me at his House. I suppose no one could have had their time made smoother than mine has been.

Lower down on the same page, instead of the words "I am going to domesticate with Brown," the original letter reads "With Dilke and Brown I am quite thick—with Brown indeed I am going to domesticate." In the second line at page 266 the word "passage" should be substituted for "page"; and the paragraph, instead of closing with "in the same room" proceeds thus in the holograph:—

I saw your Mother the day before yesterday, and intend now frequently to pass half a day with her—she seem'd tolerably well. I called in Henrietta Street and so was speaking with your Mother about Miss Millar— we had a chat about Heiresses—she told me I think of 7 or eight dying swains. Charles was not at home. I think I have heard a little more talk about Miss Keasle. All I know of her is she had a new sort of shoe on of bright leather like our knapsacks. Miss Millar gave me one of her confounded pinches. N. B. did not like it.

Mrs. Dilke went with me to see Fanny last week, and Haslam went with me last Sunday. She was well—she gets a little plumper and had a little Colour. On Sunday I brought from her a present of facescreens and a work bag for Mrs. D. They were really very pretty. From Walthamstow we walked to Bethnal green—w[h]ere I felt so tired from my long walk that I was obliged to go to Bed at ten. Mr. and Mrs. Keasle were there. Haslam has been excessively kind and his anxiety about you is great. I never meet him but we have some chat thereon. He is always doing me some good turn—he gave me this thin paper for the purpose of writing to you. I have been passing an hour this morning with Mr. Lewis—he wants news of you very much. Haydon was here yesterday—he amused us much by speaking of young Hopner who went with Captn Ross on a voyage of discovery to the Poles. The Ship was sometimes entirely surrounded with vast mountains and crags of ice and in a few Minutes not a particle was to be seen all round the Horizon. Once they met with so vast a Mass that they gave themselves over for lost; their last recourse was in meeting it with the Bowsp[r]it which they did and split it asunder and glided through it as it parted for a great distance—one Mile and more. Their eyes were so fatigued with the eternal dazzle and whiteness that they lay down on their backs upon deck to relieve their sight on the blue sky. Hopner describes his dreadful weariness at the continual day—the sun ever moving in a circle round above their heads—so pressing upon him that he could not rid himself of the sensation even in the dark Hold of the Ship. The Esquimaux are described as the most wretched of Beings—they float from the summer to their winter residences and back again like white Bears on the ice floats. They seem never to have washed, and so when their features move the red skin shows beneath the cracking peal of dirt. They had no notion of any inhabitants in the World but themselves. The sailors who had not seen a star for some time, when they came again southwards on the hailing of the first revision of one all ran upon deck with feelings of the most joyful nature. Haydon's eyes will not suffer him to proceed with his Picture—his Physician tells him he must remain two months more, inactive. Hunt keeps on in his old way—I am completely tired of it all. He has lately publish'd a Pocket Book called the literary Pocket-Book—full of the most sickening stuff you can imagine. Reynolds is well—he has become an Edinburgh Reviewer.

I have not heard from Bail[e]y. Rice I have seen very little of lately—and I am very sorry for it. The Miss Rs are all as usual. Archer above all people called on me one day—he wanted some information by my means, from Hunt and Haydon, concerning some Man they knew. I got him what he wanted but know none of the whys and wherefores. Poor Kirkman left Wentworth place one evening about half past eight and was stopped, beaten and robbed of his Watch in Pond Street. I saw him a few days since—he had not recovered from his bruize. I called on Hazlitt the day I went to Romney Street—I gave John Hunt extracts from your letters—he has taken no notice. I have seen Lamb lately—Brown and I were taken by Hunt to Novello's—there we were devastated and excruciated with bad and repeated puns. Brown don't want to go again. We went the other evening to see Brutus a new Tragedy by Howard Payne, an American—Kean was excellent—the play was very bad. It is the first time I have been since I went with you to the Lyceum.

Mrs. Brawne who took Brown's house for the summer

still resides in Hampstead—she is a very nice woman—and her daughter senior is I think beautiful and elegant, graceful, silly, fashionable and strange—we have a little tiff now and then—and she behaves a little better, or I must have sheered off. I find by a sidelong report from your Mother that I am to be invited to Miss Millar's birthday dance. Shall I dance with Miss Waldegrave? Eh! I shall be obliged to shirk a good many there. I shall be the only Dandy there—and indeed I merely comply with the invitation that the party may not be entirely destitute of a specimen of that race. I shall appear in a complete dress of purple Hat and all—with a list of the beauties I have conquered embroidered round my Calves.

The next new section in the original letter begins— "Thursday. This morning is so very fine, I should have walked over to Walthamstow if I had thought of it yesterday—" *and not in the manner shown at page* 266; *and lower down, after the question as to pointers, comes this other,* "Have you seen Mr. Trimmer? He is an acquaintance of Peachey's."

In recounting the Jane Porter incident of pages 266-7, *Keats quotes in full a letter from Woodhouse which has been ignored hitherto, a few words only being incorporated in what has purported to be Keats's own, so as to make Mr. Neville figure as a friend of the poet instead of as a friend of Woodhouse. After the allusion to a £25 note sent anonymously, the holograph reads thus:—*

I have many things to tell you—the best way will be to make copies of my correspondence; and I must not forget the Sonnet I received with the Note.—Last Week I received the following from Woodhouse whom you must recollect—"My dear Keats,—I send enclosed a

"Letter, which when read take the trouble to return to me.
"The History of its reaching me is this. My Cousin, Miss
"Frogley of Hounslow borrowed my copy of Endymion
"for a specified time. Before she had time to look into it;
"she and my friend Mr. Hy. Neville of Esher, who was
"house Surgeon to the late Princess Charlotte, insisted
"upon having it to read for a day or two, and undertook
"to make my Cousin's peace with me on account of the
"extra delay. Neville told me that one of the Misses
"Porter (of romance Celebrity) had seen it on his table,
"dipped into it, and expressed a wish to read it. I desired
"he should keep it as long and lend it to as many as he
"pleased, provided it was not allowed to slumber on any
"one's shelf. I learned subsequently from Miss Frogley
"that these Ladies had requested of Mr. Neville, if he was
"acquainted with the Author, the Pleasure of an introduc-
"tion. About a week back the enclosed was transmitted
"by Mr. Neville to my Cousin, as a species of Apology for
"keeping her so long without the Book and she sent it to
"me, knowing that it would give me Pleasure—I forward
"it to you for somewhat the same reason, but principally
"because it gives me the opportunity of naming to you
"(which it would have been fruitless to do before) the
"opening there is for an introduction to a class of society
"from which you may possibly derive advantage, as well
"as gratification, if you think proper to avail yourself of
"it. In such a case I should be very happy to further
"your Wishes. But do just as you please. The whole is
"entirely entre nous—Your's &c. R. W." Well—now
this is Miss Porter's Letter to Neville.

Keats then gives the letter of Miss Porter without much variation from the published text down to "when life is granted"; but from that point the text must have been re-

stored from another source, probably Miss Porter's actual letter; for Keats dismisses it unfinished with "'when Life is granted &c.'—and so she goes on." *His comment, immediately following the letter, on the proposed new introductions has also been mercilessly tampered with: it reads as follows in the holograph:—*

Now I feel more obliged than flattered by this—so obliged that I will not at present give you an extravaganza of a Lady Romancer. I will be introduced to them if it be merely for the pleasure of writing to you about it—I shall certainly see a new race of People. I shall more certainly have no time for them. Hunt has asked me to meet Tom Moore some day—so you shall hear of him. The Night we went to Novello's there was a complete set to of Mozart and punning. I was so completely tired of it that if I were to follow my own inclinations I should never meet any one of that set again, not even Hunt who is certainly a pleasant fellow in the main when you are with him—but in reality he is vain, egotistical, and disgusting in matters of taste and in morals. He understands many a beautiful thing; but then, instead of giving other minds credit for the same degree of perception as he himself professes—he begins an explanation in such a curious manner that our taste and self-love is offended continually. Hunt does one harm by making fine things petty and beautiful things hateful. Through him I am indifferent to Mozart, I care not for white Busts—and many a glorious thing when associated with him becomes a nothing. This distort's one's mind—makes one's thoughts bizarre—perplexes one in the standard of Beauty. Martin is very much irritated against Blackwood for printing some letters in his Magazine which were Martin's property—he always found excuses for Blackwood till he himself was injured and now he is enraged. I have been several times thinking whether or not I should send you the Examiners as Birkbeck no doubt has all the good periodical Publications—I will save them at all events. I must not forget to mention how attentive and useful Mrs. Bentley has been—I am very sorry to leave her—but I must and I hope she will not be much a loser by it—Bentley is very well—he has just brought me a cloathe's basket of Books. Brown has gone to town today to take his Nephews who are on a visit here to see the Lions.

The next new section of this long letter,—that headed " Friday" at page 268,—shows in the holograph the following unpublished passage after the words " on the next sheet" :—

I shall dine with Haydon on Sunday and go over to Walthamstow on Monday if the frost hold. I think also of going into Hampshire this Christmas to Mr. Snook's— they say I shall be very much amused. But I don't know—I think I am in too huge a Mind for study—I must do it—I must wait at home and let those who wish come to see me. I cannot always be (how do you spell it ?) trapsing. Here I must tell you that I have not been able to keep the journal or write the Tale I promised— now I shall be able to do so.

Again at the same page, between " even across the Atlantic" and " Shall I give you Miss ———" we have to insert new matter :—

But now I must speak particularly to you my dear Sister—for I know you love a little quizzing, better than a great bit of apple dumpling. Do you know Uncle Redall ? He is a little man with an innocent powdered upright head, he lisps with a protruded underlip—he has two Nieces each one would weigh three of him—one for height and the other for breadth—he knew Bartolozzi. He gave a supper and ranged his bottles of wine all up the kitchen and cellar stairs—quite ignorant of what might be drank—it might have been a good joke to pour on the sly bottle after bottle into a washing tub and roar for more. If you were to trip him up it would discompose a Pigtail and bring his under lip nearer to his nose. He never had the good luck to loose a silk Handkerchief in a Crowd and therefore has only one topic of conversation—Bartolozzi.

Then comes the fine sketch of Miss Brawne; and here the holograph is invaluable, as it sets at rest for ever any doubts which might linger as to the identity of the original, by opening clearly with the words " Shall I give you Miss Brawne ? " *In this same passage Keats himself underlines the emphatic word* " Minx " (*page* 269), *and in describing the obnoxious person whom Miss Brawne, and she only, admired or professed to admire, he makes use of some phrases which were judiciously enough omitted in the first impressions of the letter, though there is no longer any need to omit them. Thus, after* "*you have known plenty such*", *he says* " her face is raw as if she was standing out in a frost—her lips raw and seem always ready for a Pullet." *The identity of this young person is also established, indirectly. Mr. Dilke* (*see foot-note, page* 269) *had suggested that the reference might be to a Miss Robinson: it was; for, after the phrase* " *superiour as a rose to a Dandelion* ", *the holograph reads—*

When we went to bed Brown observed as he put out the Taper what a very ugly old woman that Miss Robinson would make—at which I must have groaned aloud for I'm sure ten minutes. I have not seen the thing

Kingston again—George will describe him to you—I shall insinuate some of these Creatures into a Comedy some day—and perhaps have Hunt among them.—Scene, a little Parlour—Enter Hunt—Gattie—Hazlitt—Mrs. Novello—Ollier. *Gattie*:—"Ha! Hunt got into your new house? Ha! Mrs. Novello: seen Altam and his wife? *Mrs. N.* Yes (with a grin): it's Mr. Hunt's isn't it? *Gattie*: Hunt's? no, ha! Mr. Ollier I congratulate you upon the highest compliment I ever heard paid to the Book. Mr Hazlitt, I hope you are well. *Hazlitt*:—Yes Sir, no Sir—*Mr. Hunt* (at the Music) "La Biondina" &c.—Hazlitt, did you ever hear this?—"La Biondina" &c. *Hazlitt*:—O no Sir—I never— *Ollier*:—Do Hunt give it us over again—divine— — *Gattie*: divino—Hunt when does your Pocket-Book come out— *Hunt*:—"What is this absorbs me quite?" O we are spinning on a little, we shall floridize soon I hope. Such a thing was very much wanting—people think of nothing but money getting—now for me I am rather inclined to the liberal side of things. I am reckoned lax in my christian principles &c. &c. &c.

It is some days since I wrote the last page—and what have I been about since I have no Idea—I dined at Haslam's on Sunday—with Haydon yesterday and saw Fanny in the morning—she was well—Just now I took out my poem to go on with it—but the thought of my writing so little to you came upon me and I could not get on—so I have began at random and I have not a word to say—and yet my thoughts are so full of you that I can do nothing else. I shall be confined at Hampstead a few days on account of a sore throat—the first thing I do will be to visit your Mother again. The last time I saw Henry he show'd me his first engraving which I thought capital. Mr. Lewis called this morning and brought some American Papers. I have not looked into them. I think we ought to have heard of you before this—I am in daily expectation of Letters—Nil desperandum. Mrs. Abbey wishes to take Fanny from School—I shall strive all I can against that. There has happened a great Misfortune in the Drewe Family—old Drewe has been dead some time; and lately George Drewe expired in a fit—on which account Reynolds has gone into Devonshire. He dined a few days since at Horace Twisse's with Liston and Charles Kemble. I see very little of him now, as I seldom go to Little Britain because the Ennui always seizes me there, and John Reynolds is very dull at home. Nor have I seen Rice. How you are now going on is a Mystery to me—I hope a few days will clear it up. I never know the day of the Month. It is very fine here to-day though I expect a Thundercloud or rather a snow cloud in less than an hour. I am at present alone at Wentworth place—Brown being at Chichester and Mr. and Mrs. Dilke making a little stay in Town. I know not what I should do without a sunshiny morning now and then—it clear's up one's spirits. Dilke and I frequently have some chat about you. I have now and then some doubt; but he seems to have great confidence. I think there will soon be perceptible a change in the fashionable slang literature of the day—it seems to me that Reviews have had their day—that the public have been surfeited—there will soon be some new folly to keep the Parlours in talk. What it is I care not. We have seen three literary Kings in our Time—Scott—Byron—and then the Scotch novels.[1]

---

[1] It is interesting to observe that Keats, at all events, had not fathomed Sir Walter Scott's secret; and it will be seen later on (page 118) that the professional critic Hazlitt was in the same case.

All now appears to be dead—or I may mistake—literary Bodies may still keep up the Bustle which I do not hear. Haydon show'd me a letter he had received from Tripoli—Ritchie was well and in good Spirits, among Camels, Turbans, Palm Trees and Sands. —You may remember I promised to send him an Endymion which I did not—however he has one—you have one.—One is in the Wilds of America—the other is on a Camel's back in the plains of Egypt.

It will be seen from the foregoing that the new section begun at the top of page 270 had been properly retrenched but very improperly manipulated. Only a few words of the passage will be found in the old text, and those inaccurately given by way of introduction to the account of Dubois's book. Of the following passage, which in the original letter comes after the sonnet and £25 note episode (page 271), only a few words were extracted in the Jeffrey-Houghton text, namely those about the Tomtit shooting on Hampstead Heath, and "Thursday—On my word, I think so little, I have not one opinion except in matters of taste,"—which are wrong:—

I have your Miniature on the Table George the great —it's very like—though not quite about the upper lip. I wish we had a better of you, little George. I must not forget to tell you that a few days since I went with Dilke a shooting on the heath and shot a Tomtit. There were as many guns abroad as Birds. I intended to have been at Chichester this Wednesday—but on account of this sore throat I wrote him (Brown) my excuse yesterday.

Thursday. I will date when I finish—I received a note from Haslam yesterday asking if my letter is ready —now this is only the second sheet—notwithstanding all my promises. But you must reflect what hindrances I have had. However on sealing this I shall have nothing to prevent my proceeding in a gradual journal which will increase in a Month to a considerable size. I will insert any little pieces I may write—though I will not give any extracts from my large poem which is scarce began. I want to hear very much whether Poetry and literature in general has gained, or lost interest with you, and what sort of writing is of the highest gust with you now. With what sensation do you read Fielding? and do not Hogarth's pictures seem an old thing to you? Yet you are very little more removed from general association than I am—recollect that no Man can live but in one society at a time—his enjoyment in the different states of human society must depend upon the Powers of his Mind—that is you can imagine a Roman triumph or an olympic game as well as I can. We with our bodily eyes see but the fashion and Manners of one country for one age—and then we die. Now to me manners and customs long since passed whether among the Babylonians or the Bactrians are as real, or even more real than those among which I now live. My thoughts have turned lately this way. The more we know the more inadequacy we find in the world to satisfy us—this is an old observation; but I have made up my Mind never to take anything for granted—but even to examine the truth of the commonest proverbs. This however is true—Mrs. Tighe and Beattie once delighted me—now I see through them and can find nothing in them or weakness, and yet how many they still delight! Perhaps a superior being may look upon Shakespeare in the same light—is it possible? No—This same inadequacy is discovered (forgive me little George—you know I don't mean to put you in the mess) in Women with few exceptions—the Dress Maker, the blue Stocking and the most charming sentimentalist differ but in a slight degree and are equally smokeable. But I'll go no further I may be speaking sacrilegeously—and on my word I have thought so little that I have not one opinion upon any thing except in matters of taste.

We have been sadly in need of a few correct and full dates for this letter; and here at last the holograph yields one,—the allusion to Hazlitt's lectures (page 272) being followed immediately by this passage—

Saturday Jan.ʸ 2nd. [1819] Yesterday Mr. and Mrs. D. and myself dined at Mrs. Brawne's—nothing particular passed. I never intend hereafter to spend any time with ladies unless they are handsome—you lose time to no purpose. For that reason I shall beg leave to decline going again to Redall's or Butler's or any Squad where a fine feature cannot be mustered among them all—and where all the evening's amusement consists in saying your good health, *your* good health, and YOUR good health—and (O I beg your pardon) yours Miss — — and such thing [*sic*] not even dull enough to keep me awake—with respect to amiable speaking I can read—let my eyes be fed or I'll never go out to dinner anywhere. Perhaps you may have heard of the dinner given to Thos. Moore in Dublin, because I have the account here by me in the Philadelphia democratic paper. The most pleasant thing that occur[r]ed was the speech Mr. Tom made on his Father's health being drank. I am afraid a great part of my Letters are filled up with promises and what I will do rather than any great deal written—but here I say once for all—that circumstances prevented me from keeping my promise in my last, but now I affirm that as there will be nothing to hinder me I will keep a journal for you. That I have not yet done so you would forgive if you knew how many hours I have been repenting of my neglect. For I have no thought pervading me so constantly and frequently as that of you—my Poem cannot frequently drive it away—you will retard it much more than you could by taking up my time if you were in England. I never forget you except after seeing now and then some beautiful woman —but that is a fever—the thought of you both is a passion with me but for the most part a calm one. I asked Dilke for a few lines for you—he has promised them—I shall send what I have written to Haslam on Monday Morning—what I can get into another sheet tomorrow I will—there are one or two little poems you might like. I have given up snuff very nearly quite—Dilke has promised to sit with me this evening—I wish he would come this minute for I want a pinch of snuff very much just now—I have none though in my own snuffbox. My sore throat is much better to day—I think I might venture on a pinch.

Here are the Poems—they will explain themselves— as all poems should do without any comment

Ever let the Fancy roam, &c.[1]

I did not think this had been so long a Poem. I have another not so long—but as it will more conveniently be copied on the other side I will just put down here some observations on Caleb Williams by Hazlitt—I meant to say St. Leon, for although he has mentioned all the Novels of Godwin very freely I do not quote them; but this only on account of its being a specimen of his usual abrupt manner and fiery laconicism. He says of St.

---

[1] See Volume II, pages 122 to 126.

Leon "He is a limb torn off society. In possession of
" eternal youth and beauty he can feel no love; sur-
" rounded, tantalized and tormented with riches, he can
" do no good. The faces of Men pass before him as in a
" speculum ; but he is attached to them by no common
" tie of sympathy or suffering. He is thrown back into
" himself and his own thoughts. He lives in the solitude
" of his own breast—without wife or child or friend or
" Enemy in the world. *This is the solitude of the soul,*
" *not of woods or trees or mountains*—but the desert of
" society—the waste and oblivion of the heart. He is
" himself alone. His existence is purely intellectual, and
" is therefore intolerable to one who has felt the rapture
" of affection, or the anguish of woe." As I am about it
I might as well give you his character of Godwin as a
Romancer "Whoever else is, it is pretty clear that the
" author of Caleb Williams is not the Author of Waverley.
" Nothing can be more distinct or excellent in their
" several ways than these two writers. If the one owes
" almost everything to external observations and tradi-
" tional character, the other owes everything to internal
" conception and contemplation of the possible workings
" of the human Mind. There is little knowledge of the
" world, little variety, neither an eye for the picturesque
" nor a talent for the humourous in Caleb Williams, for
" instance, but you cannot doubt for a moment of the
" originality of the work and the force of the conception.
" The impression made upon the reader is the exact
" measure of the strength of the author's genius. For
" the effect both in Caleb Williams and St. Leon is
" entirely made out, not by facts nor dates, by blackletter,
" or magazine learning, by transcript nor record, but by
" intense and patient study of the human heart, and by
" an imagination projecting itself into certain situations,

" and capable of working up its imaginary feelings to
" the height of reality." This appears to me quite correct
—now I will copy the other Poem—it is on the double
immortality of Poets—

> Bards of Passion and of Mirth, &c.[1]

These are specimens of a sort of rondeau which I
think I shall become partial to—because you have one
idea amplified with greater ease and more delight and
freedom than in the sonnet. It is my intention to wait
a few years before I publish any minor poems—and then
I hope to have a volume of some worth—and which
those people will relish who cannot bear the burthen of
a long poem. In my journal I intend to copy the
poems I write the days they are written—there is just
room I see in this page to copy a little thing I wrote off
to some Music as it was playing—

> I had a dove and the sweet dove died, &c.[2]

Sunday [3 January 1819]. I have been dining with
Dilke to day—He is up to his Ears in Walpole's letters.
Mr. Manker[3] is there; I have come round to see if I
can conjure up anything for you. Kirkman came down
to see me this morning—his family has been very badly
off lately. He told me of a villainous trick of his Uncle
William in Newgate Street who became sole Creditor to
his father under pretence of serving him, and put an
execution on his own sister's goods. He went into the
family at Portsmouth; conversed with them, went out and
sent in the Sheri[f]f's officer. He tells me too of abomi-
nable behaviour of Archer to Caroline Mathew—Archer
has lived nearly at the Mathews these two years; he

---

[1] See Volume II, pages 127 to 129.   [2] See Volume II, page 281.
[3] Probably identical with the "Mancur" of page 148.

has been amusing Caroline—and now he has written a Letter to Mrs. M. declining on pretence of inability to support a wife as he would wish, all thoughts of marriage. What is the worst is Caroline is 27 years old. It is an abominable matter. He has called upon me twice lately—I was out both times. What can it be for—There is a letter to day in the Examiner to the Electors of Westminster on Mr. Hobhouse's account.[1] In it there is a good character of Cobbet[t]—I have not the paper by me or I would copy it. I do not think I have mentioned the discovery of an African kingdom—the account is much the same as the first accounts of Mexico—all magnificence—there is a Book being written about it. I will read it and give you the cream in my next. The romance we have heard upon it runs thus: they have window frames of gold—100,000 infantry—human sacrifices. The gentleman who is the Adventurer has his wife with him—she I am told is a beautiful little sylphid woman—her husband was to have been sacrificed to their Gods and was led through a Chamber filled with different instruments of torture with privelege to choose what death he would die, without their having a thought of his aversion to such a death—they considering it a supreme distinction. However he was let off and became a favorite with the King who at last openly patronized him, though at first on account of the Jealousy of his Ministers he was wont to hold conversations with his Majesty in the dark middle of the night. All this sounds a little Blue-beardish—but I hope it is true. There is another thing I must mention of the

---

[1] It is this allusion that fixes the particular Sunday and shows that the writing had not been broken off for a week. The letter referred to is in *The Examiner* for the 3rd of January 1819.

momentous kind ;—but I must mind my periods in it—Mrs. Dilke has two Cats—a Mother and a Daughter—now the Mother is a tabby and the daughter a black and white like the spotted child. Now it appears to me for the doors of both houses are opened frequently—so that there is a complete thoroughfare for both Cats (there being no board up to the contrary) they may one and several of them come into my room ad libitum. But no—the Tabby only comes—whether from sympathy from Ann the Maid or me I cannot tell—or whether Brown has left behind him atmospheric spirit of Maidenhood I cannot tell. The Cat is not an old Maid herself—her daughter is a proof of it—I have questioned her—I have look'd at the lines of her paw—I have felt her pulse—to no purpose. Why should the old Cat come to me? I ask myself—and myself has not a word to answer. It may come to light some day; if it does you shall hear of it.

The next and final paragraph in the original letter has been so maltreated in previously published texts that I have no alternative but to give the opening and close here: it begins thus—

Kirkman this morning promised to write a few lines to you and send them to Haslam. I do not think I have anything to say in the Business way. You will let me know what you would wish done with your property in England—what things you would wish sent out—but I am quite in the dark about what you are doing—if I do not hear soon I shall put on my wings and be after you. I will in my next, and after I have seen your next letter tell you my own particular idea of America. Your next letter will be the key by which I shall open your hearts and see what spaces want filling with any particular information.

122 ADDITIONAL PROSE WRITINGS.

The reasons for materially altering the facts by representing that Keats was unaware of his brother's arrival in America, and had not heard from him (see page 272), are anything but obvious; though there may have been some colourable excuse for improving the grammar of the account of Miss Millar's lovers, which in the holograph ends thus—

The ninth stuck to her mother—the tenth kissed the Chambermaid and told her to tell her Mistress—But he was soon discharged—his reading lead him into an error—he could not sport the Sir Lucius to any advantage.

The end of the letter is not that of the Jeffrey-Houghton version, but this:

And now for this time I bid you goodby—I have been thin[kin]g of these sheets so long that I appear in closing them to take my leave of you—but that is not it—I shall immediately as I send this off begin my journal—when some days I shall write no more than 10 lines and others 10 times as much. Mrs. Dilke is knocking at the wall for Tea is ready—I will tell you what sort of a tea it is and then bid you—Good bye—This is monday morning[1]—nothing particular happened yesterday evening, except that when the tray came up Mrs. Dilke and I had a battle with celery stalks—she sends her love to you. I shall close this and send it immediately to Haslam—remaining ever

    My dearest brother and sister
    Your most affectionate Brother
      John—

The American editor makes considerable additions to the

---

[1] The 4th of January 1819.

long and important journal-letter to George and Georgiana Keats begun on the 14th of February 1819, printed at pages 274 to 286 of Volume III, and numbered LXXXVI; and indeed he would seem to have seen the manuscript of a small portion. Of the greater part the autograph is in England, and has been consulted for the purposes of this book. The earlier part of this document was greatly retrenched and altered when first published by Lord Houghton. Mr. Speed says that his grandmother's second husband, who transcribed it for Lord Houghton, did not exercise a very wise discretion in his manipulations; and certainly there was some lack of judgment somewhere; for, in previous versions, the reference, made near the beginning, to the second place at which Keats and Brown had been staying in Hampshire is cut out, and the statement that "nothing worth speaking of happened AT EITHER PLACE" *is left standing—without mark of omission. The first part of the letter now stands thus:—*

Sunday Morn, Feby. 14th 1819.

My Dear Brother and Sister:

How is it we have not heard from you from the Settlement yet? The letters must surely have miscarried. I am in expectation every day. Peachey wrote me a few days ago, saying some more acquaintances of his were preparing to set out for Birkbeck; therefore, I shall take the opportunity of sending you what I can muster in a sheet or two. I am still at Wentworth Place—indeed, I have kept indoors lately, resolved if possible to rid myself of my sore throat; consequently, I have not been to see your mother since my return from Chichester; but my absence from her has been a great weight upon me. I say since my return from Chichester —I believe I told you I was going thither. I was nearly a fortnight at Mr. John Snooks's,[1] and a few days at old Mr. Dilke's. Nothing worth speaking of happened at either place. I took down some thin paper and wrote on it a little poem call'd "St. Agnes' Eve," which you shall have as it is when I have finished the blank part of the rest for you. I went out twice at Chichester to old dowager card parties. I see very little now, and very few persons, being almost tired of men and things. Brown and Dilke are very kind and considerate towards me. The Miss R——s[2] have been stopping next door lately, but are very dull. Miss Brawne and I have every now and then a chat and a tiff. Brown and Dilke are walking round their garden, hands in pockets, making observations. The literary world I know nothing about. There is a poem from Rogers[3] dead born; and another satire is expected from Byron, called "Don Giovanni." Yesterday I went to town for the first time for these three weeks. I met people from all parts and of all sets —Mr. Towers,[4] one of the Holts, Mr. Dominie Williams, Mr. Woodhouse, Mrs. Hazlitt and son, Mrs. Webb, and Mrs. Septimus Brown. Mr. Woodhouse was looking up at a book window in Newgate street, and, being short-sighted, twisted his muscles into so queer a stage that I stood by in doubt whether it was him or his brother, if he

---

[1] This should of course be *Snook's*. The mistake may have been Keats's own; but it would be unsafe in the circumstances to assume that he is responsible for the improvement of his friend's name.

[2] Probably Keats did not indicate any further who the friends were; for it is scarcely credible that Mr. Speed would have any delicacy about naming them if he knew them.

[3] *Human Life*.

[4] Charles Cowden Clarke had lodged at the house of a Mr. Towers, in Warner Street, Clerkenwell.

has one, and turning round, saw Mrs. Hazlitt, with that little Nero, her son.[1]

The following passage, almost all fresh, Mr. Speed interpolates after "till I hear from you" (page 275, third volume, line 6 from foot) :—

I am invited to Miss Millar's birthday dance on the 19th. I am nearly sure I shall not be able to go. A dance would injure my throat very much. I see very little of Reynolds. Hunt, I hear is going on very badly —I mean in money matters. I shall not be surprised to hear of the worst. Haydon, too, in consequence of his eyes, is out at elbows. I live as prudently as it is possible for me to do. I have not seen Haslam lately. I have not seen Richards for this half year, Rice for three months, or Charles Cowden Clarke for God knows when.

When I last called in Henrietta street, Miss Millar was very unwell, and Miss Waldegrave as staid and self-possessed as usual. Henry was well. There are two new tragedies—one by the apostate Maw, and one by Miss Jane Porter. Next week I am going to stop at Taylor's for a few days, when I will see them both and tell you what they are. Mr. and Mrs. Bentley are well, and all the young carrots. I said nothing of consequence passed at Snooks's [2]—no more than this—that I like the family very much. Mr. and Mrs. Snooks [2] were very kind. We used to have a little religion and politicks to-

---

[1] This seems more likely to be right than the old version, " saw Mr. Hazlitt, with his son." See page 275, where also Woodhouse figures as twisting his muscles into " so queer a *style*," which is certainly more likely to be what Keats wrote than *stage*, though *shape* is likelier still.

[2] See note at page 124.

gether almost every evening,—and sometimes about you. He proposed writing out for me his experience in farming, for me to send to you. If I should have an opportunity of talking to him about it, I will get all I can at all events; but you may say in your answer to this what value you place upon such information. I have not seen Mr. Lewis lately, for I have shrunk from going up the hill. Mr. Lewis went a few mornings ago to town with Mrs. Brawne. They talked about me, and I heard that Mr. L. said a thing that I am not at all contented with. Says he, "O, he is quite the little poet."[1] Now this is abominable. You might as well say Buonaparte is quite the little soldier. You see what it is to be under six foot and not a lord. There is a long fuzz to-day in the "Examiner" about a young man who delighted a young woman with a valentine. I think it must be Ollier's. Brown and I are thinking of passing the summer at Brussels. If we do, we shall go about the first of May. We—*i.e.*, Brown and I—sit opposite one another all day authorizing. (N.B., an "s" instead of a "z" would give a different meaning.[2]) He is at present writing a story of an old woman who lived in a forest, and to whom the devil or one of his aid-de-feus came one night very late and in disguise. The old dame sets before him pudding after pudding,—mess after mess,—which he devours, and moreover casts his eyes up at a side of bacon hanging

---

[1] These last two lines, though new as now given, are represented at page 275 by the following :—" Mrs. S. met me the other day. I heard she said a thing I am not at all content with. Says she, 'O, he is quite the little poet.'" For the next three lines see page 275.

[2] I suppose Keats meant that the word *authorising*, spelt as printers generally choose to spell all such words, would have its usual sense, and thought he had sufficiently differentiated it into a cognate meaning with *philosophizing, poetizing*, &c., by employing a *z*,—a curious delusion enough.

over his head, and at the same time asks whether her cat is a rabbit. On going, he leaves her three pips of Eve's apple,[1] and somehow she, having lived a virgin all her life, begins to repent of it, and wished herself beautiful enough to make all the world and even the other world fall in love with her. So it happens, she sets out from her smokey cottage in magnificent apparel. The first city she enters, every one falls in love with her, from the prince to the blacksmith. A young gentleman on his way to the church to be married leaves his unfortunate bride and follows this nonsuch. A whole regiment of soldiers are smitten at once and follow her. A whole convent of monks in Corpus Christi procession join the soldiers. The mayor and corporation follow the same road. Old and young, deaf and dumb—all but the blind,—are smitten, and form an immense concourse of people, who—what Brown will do with them I know not. The devil himself falls in love with her, flies away with her to a desert place, in consequence of which she lays an infinite number of eggs. The eggs, being hatched from time to time, fill the world with many nuisances, such as John Knox, George Fox, Johanna Southcote, and Gifford.

There have been within a fortnight eight failures of the highest consequence in London. Brown went a few evenings since to Davenport's, and on his coming in he talked about bad news in the city with such a face I began to think of a national bankruptcy. I did not feel much surprised and was rather disappointed. Carlisle,

---

[1] The curious poem *Sharing Eve's Apple* (Volume II, page 279) may perhaps be connected in its origin with this story of Brown's,—the sharing of the apple being, in the poem, incompatible with virginity. If so, the date of the poem may perhaps be 1819 instead of 1818.

a bookseller on the *Hone* principle, has been issuing pamphlets from his shop in Fleet street called the Deïst. He was conveyed to Newgate last Thursday; he intends making his own defense. I was surprised to hear from Taylor the amount of money [1] of the booksellers' last sale. What think you of £25,000? He sold 4000 copies of Lord Byron. I am sitting opposite the Shakspeare I brought from the isle of Wight—and I never look at it but the silk tassels on it give me as much pleasure as the face of the poet itself.

Mr. Speed gives another fresh passage between the words "I must wait for the spring to rouse me a little" (page 276) and the paragraph beginning with the date "Friday, 19th February [1819]." The interpolation is as follows:—

The only time I went out from Bedhampton was to see a chapel consecrated. Brown, I, and John Snook the boy,[2] went in a chaise behind a leaden horse. Brown drove, but the horse did not mind him. This chapel is built by a Mr. Way,[3] a great Jew converter, who in that line has spent one hundred thousand pounds. He maintains a great number of poor Jews. *Of course, his communion-plate was stolen.* He spoke to the clerk about it. The clerk said he was very sorry, adding: "*I dare shay, your honour, it's among ush.*"

---

[1] Probably a mistake of the American editor: the real words are likely to be "the amount of Murray the bookseller's last sale."

[2] Mr. John Snook of Belmont Castle ("the boy") died on the 1st of February 1887.

[3] From Brown's part of the joint letter written by him and Keats to Mr. and Mrs. Dilke on the 24th of January 1819 (page 262), it appears that the consecration was fixed for the 25th, to be performed by the Bishops of Gloucester and St. Davids, and that the chapel was at a place called Sanstead.

The chapel is built in Mr. Way's park. The consecration was not amusing. There were numbers of carriages —and his house crammed with clergy. They sanctified the chapel, and it being a wet day, consecrated the burial-ground through the vestry window. I begin to hate parsons; they did not make me love them that day, when I saw them in their proper colours. A parson is a lamb in a drawing-room and a lion in a vestry. The notions of society will not permit a parson to give way to his temper in any shape—so he festers in himself—his features get a peculiar, diabolical, self-sufficient, iron stupid expression. He is continually acting. His mind is against every man, and every man's mind is against him. He is an hypocrite to the believer and a coward to the unbeliever. He must be either a knave or an idiot—and there is no man so much to be pitied as an idiot parson. The soldier who is cheated into an *esprit du corps*[1] by a red coat, a band, and colours, for the purpose of nothing, is not half so pitiable as the parson who is led by the nose by the bench of bishops and is smothered in absurdities—a poor, necessary subaltern of the Church.

The paragraph headed " Friday, 19th February [1819]" at page 276 of the third volume opens thus in the original letter:—

Friday Feby 18.—The day before yesterday I went to Romney Street—your Mother was not at home—but I have just written her that I shall see her on wednesday.

---

[1] It is impossible, in the absence of the manuscript, to say whether Keats, whose French was certainly not particularly good, is indebted or not to his brother's grandson for the unfortunate turn of this phrase.

I call'd on Mr. Lewis this morning—he is very well—and tells me not to be uneasy about Letters the chances being so arbit[r]ary. He is going on as usual among his favorite democrat papers. We had a chat as usual about Cobbett and the Westminster electors. Dilke has lately been very much harassed about the manner of educating his son—he at length decided for a public school—and then he did not know what school—he at last has decided for Westminster; and as Charley is to be a day boy, Dilke will remove to Westminster.

There are many minute variations from the published versions in what follows the above; and after the allusion to a pheasant given to Mrs. Dilke (page 277) we read " on which tomorrow Rice, Reynolds and the Wentworthians will dine next door." *Then, after " The next I intend for your Mother," comes this :—*

These moderate sheets of paper are much more pleasant to write upon than those large thin sheets which I hope you by this time have received—though that can't be now I think of it.

After " who wins or who loses " in the last line but one of page 277 stands the following passage:

Brown is going on this morning with the story of his old woman and the devil. He makes but slow progress. The fact is it is a Libel on the Devil, and as that person is Brown's Muse, look ye, if he libels his own Muse how can he expect to write. Either Brown or his muse must turn tale [*sic*].

Yesterday was Charley Dilke's birthday. Brown and I were invited to tea. During the evening nothing passed worth notice but a little conversation between

Mrs. Dilke and Mrs. Brawne. The subject was the Watchman. It was ten o'Clock and Mrs. Brawne who lived during the summer in Brown's house and now lives in the Road, recognized her old Watchman's voice and said that he came as far as her now: "indeed" said Mrs. D. "does he turn the Corner?" There have been some Letters pass between me and Haslam but I have not seen him lately—the day before yesterday—which I made a day of Business—I called upon him—he was out as usual. Brown has been walking up and down the room a breeding—now at this moment he is being delivered of a couplet—and I dare say will be as well as can be expected.—Gracious—he has twins! I have a long story to tell you about Bailey—I will say first the circumstances as plainly and as well as I can remember and then I will make my comment. You know that Bailey was very much cut up about a little Jilt in the country somewhere. I thought he was in a dying state about it when at Oxford with him: little supposing as I have since heard that he was at that very time making impatient Love to Marian[e] Reynolds—and guess my astonishment at hearing after this that he had been trying at Miss Martin. So matters have been. So Matters stood—when he got ordained and went to a Curacy near Carlisle where the family of the Gleigs reside. There his susceptible heart was conquered by Miss Gleig—and thereby all his connections in town have been annulled both male and female. I do not now remember clearly the facts. These however I know. He showed his correspondence with Marian[e] to Gleig—returned all her Letters and asked for his own—he also wrote very abrupt Letters to Mrs. Reynolds. I do not know any more of the Martin affair than I have written above. No doubt his conduct has been very bad. The great thing to be considered is—whether it is want of delicacy and principle or want of knowledge and polite experience. And again weakness—yes that is it—and the want of a Wife—yes that is it—and then Marian[e] made great Bones of him although her Mother and sister have teased her very much about it. Her conduct has been very upright throughout the whole affair—She liked Bailey as a Brother but not as a Husband—especially as he used to woo her with the Bible and Jeremy Taylor under his arm—they walked in no grove but Jeremy Taylor's. Marian[e]'s obstinacy is some excuse—but his so quickly taking to Miss Gleig can have no excuse—except that of a Ploughman who wants a wife. The thing which sways me more against him than anything else is Rice's conduct on the occasion; Rice would not make an immature resolve: he was ardent in his friendship for Bailey, he examined the whole for and against minutely; and he has abandoned Bailey entirely. All this I am not supposed by the Reynoldses to have any hint of. It will be a good lesson to the Mother and Daughters—nothing would serve but Bailey. If you mentioned the word Teapot some one of them came out with an à propos about Bailey—noble fellow—fine fellow! was always in their mouths—this may teach them that the man who ridicules romance is the most romantic of Men—that he who abuses women and slights them—loves them the most—that he who talks of roasting a Man alive would not do it when it came to the push—and above all that they are very shallow people who take every thing literal. A Man's life of any worth is a continual allegory—and very few eyes can see the Mystery of his life—a life like the scriptures figurative—which such people can no more make out than they can the Hebrew Bible. Lord Byron cuts a figure but he is not figurative. Shakespeare led a life of Allegory: his works are the comments on it.[1]

March 12. Friday. I went to town yesterday chiefly for the purpose of seeing some young Men who were to take some Letters for us to you—through the medium of Peachey. I was surprised and disappointed at hearing they had changed their minds and did not purpose going so far as Birkbeck's. I was much disappointed for I had counted upon seeing some persons who were to see you —and upon your seeing some who had seen me—I have not only lost this opportunity—but the sail of the Post-Packet to New York or Philadelphia—by which last your Brothers have sent some Letters. The weather in town yesterday was so stifling that I could not remain there though I wanted much to see Kean in Hotspur. I have by me at present Hazlitt's Letter to Gifford—perhaps you would like an extract or two from the high seasoned parts. It begins thus "Sir, You have an ugly trick of
" saying what is not true of any one you do not like; and
" it will be the object of this Letter to cure you of it.
" You say what you please of others; it is time you were
" told what you are. In doing this give me leave to
" borrow the familiarity of your style :—for the fidelity of
" the picture I shall be answerable. You are a little
" person but a considerable cat's paw; and so far worthy
" of notice. Your clandestine connection with persons
" high in office constantly influences your opinions and
" alone gives importance to them. You are the govern-
" ment critic, a character nicely differing from that of a
" government spy—the invisible link which connects

---

[1] This passage ends at the bottom of a page; the next words are at the top of a new page of a different sized paper; and there may possibly be something missing between them.

" literature with the Police." Again—"Your employers,
" Mr. Gifford; do not pay their hirelings for nothing—for
" condescending to notice weak and wicked sophistry; for
" pointing out to contempt what excites no admiration;
" for cautiously selecting a few specimens of bad taste and
" bad grammar where nothing else is to be found. They
" want your invincible pertness, your mercenary malice,
" your impenetrable dullness, your barefaced impudence,
" your pragmatical self-sufficiency, your hypocritical zeal,
" your pious frauds to stand in the gap of their Prejudices
" and pretensions to fly blow and taint public opinion, to
" defeat independent efforts, to apply not the touch of the
" scorpion but the touch of the Torpedo to youthful hopes,
" to crawl and leave the slimy track of sophistry and lies
" over every work that does not 'dedicate its sweet leaves'
" to some Luminary of the tre[a]sury bench, or is not
" fostered in the hot bed of corruption. This is your office;
" 'this is what is look'd for at your hands and this you do
" 'not baulk'—to sacrifice what little honesty and prosti-
" tute what little intellect you possess to any dirty job you
" are commission'd to execute. 'They keep you as an ape
" 'does an apple in the corner of his jaw, first mouth'd to
" 'be at last swallow'd.' You are by appointment literary
" toadeater to greatness and taster to the court. You have
" a natural aversion to whatever differs from your own
" pretensions, and an acquired one for what gives offence
" to your superiors. Your vanity panders to your interest
" and your malice truckles only to your love of Power. If
" your instructive or premeditated abuse of your enviable
" trust were found wanting in a single instance; if you
" were to make a single slip in getting up your select com-
" mittee of enquiry and green bag report of the state of
" Letters, your occupation would be gone. You would
" never after obtain a squeeze of the hand from a great

" man, or a smile from a Punk of Quality. The great and
" powerful (whom you call wise and good) do not like to
" have the privacy of their self love startled by the
" obtrusive and unmanageable claims of Literature and
" Philosophy, except through the intervention of people
" like you, whom, if they have common penetration, they
" soon find out to be without any superiority of intellect;
" or if they do not whom they can despise for their mean-
" ness of soul. You 'have the office opposite to saint
" ' Peter.' You keep a corner in the public mind for foul
" prejudice and corrupt power to knot and gender in; you
" volunteer your services to people of quality to ease
" scruples of mind and qualms of conscience; you lay the
" flattering unction of venal prose and laurell'd verse to
" their souls. You persuade them that there is neither
" purity of morals, nor depth of understanding except in
" themselves and their hangers on; and would prevent the
" unhallow'd names of Liberty and humanity from ever
" being whispered in ears polite! You, sir, do you not all
" this? I cry you mercy then: I took you for the Editor
" of the Quarterly Review!" This is the sort of feu de joie
he keeps up—there is another extract or two—one espe-
cially which I will copy tomorrow—for the candles are
burnt down and I am using the wax taper—which has a
long snuff on it—the fire is at its last click—I am sitting
with my back to it with one foot rather askew upon the
rug and the other with the heel a little elevated from the
carpet—I am writing this on the Maid's tragedy which I
have read since tea with Great pleasure. Besides this
volume of Beaumont and Fletcher—there are on the
table two volumes of Chaucer and a new work of Tom
Moore's called "Tom Cribb's Memorial to Congress"—
nothing in it. These are trifles but I require nothing so
much of you but that you will give me a like description

of yourselves, however it may be when you are writing to me. Could I see the same thing done of any great Man long since dead it would be a great delight: As to know in what position Shakespeare sat when he began "To be or not to be"—such things become interesting from distance of time or place. I hope you are both now in that sweet sleep which no two beings deserve more than you do—I must fancy you so—and please myself in the fancy of speaking a prayer and a blessing over you and your lives—God bless you—I whisper good night in your ears and you will dream of me.

Saturday 13 March [1819]. I have written to Fanny this morning and received a note from Haslam. I was to have dined with him tomorrow: he give[s] me a bad account of his Father who has not been in Town for 5 weeks—and is not well enough for company—Haslam is well—and from the prosperous state of some love affair he does not mind the double tides he has to work. I have been a walk past Westend—and was going to call at Mr. Monkhouse's—but I did not not being in the humour. I know not why Poetry and I have been so distant lately I must make some advances soon or she will cut me entirely. Hazlitt has this fine Passage in his Letter: Gifford in his Review of Hazlitt's characters of Shakespeare's plays attacks the Coriolanus critique. He says that Hazlitt has slandered Shakespeare in saying that he had a leaning to the arbit[r]ary side of the question. Hazlitt thus defends himself "My words
" are 'Coriolanus is a storehouse of political common-
"'places. The Arguments for and against aristocracy
"'and d[e]mocracy on the Privileges of the few and the
"'claims of the many, on Liberty and slavery, power and
"'the abuse of it, peace and war, are here very ably
"'handled, with the spirit of a Poet and the acuteness of

" ' a Philosopher. Shakespeare himself seems to have had
" ' a leaning to the arbit[r]ary side of the question, perhaps
" ' from some feeling of contempt for his own origin, and
" ' to have spared no occasion of bating the rabble. What
" ' he says of them is very true ; what he says of their
" ' betters is also very true, though he dwells less upon it.'
" I then proceed to account for this by showing how it is
" that ' the cause of the people is but little calculated for
" ' a subject for poetry ; or that the language of Poetry
" ' naturally falls in with the language of power.' I affirm,
" Sir, that Poetry, that the imagination generally speaking,
" delights in power, in strong excitement, as well as in
" truth, in good, in right, whereas pure reason and the
" moral sense approve only of the true and good. I pro-
" ceed to show that this general love or tendency to imme-
" diate excitement or theatrical effect no matter how pro-
" duced gives a Bias to the imagination often consistent
" with the greatest good, that in Poetry it triumphs over
" principle, and bribes the passions to make a sacrifice of
" common humanity. You say that it does not, that there
" is no such original Sin in Poetry, that it makes no such
" sacrifice or unworthy compromise between poetical effect
" and the still small voice of reason. And how do you
" prove that there is no such principle giving a bias to the
" imagination and a false colouring to poetry ? Why by
" asking in reply to the instances where this principle
" operates, and where no other can with much modesty and
" simplicity—' But are these the only topics that afford
" ' delight in Poetry &c.' No ; but these objects do afford
" delight in poetry, and they afford it in proportion to their
" strong and often tragical effect, and not in proportion to
" the good produced, or their desireableness in a moral
" point of view ? Do we read with more pleasure of the
" ravages of a beast of prey than of the Shepherd's pipe

" upon the Mountain? No but we do read with pleasure of
" the ravages of a beast of prey, and we do so on the principle
" I have stated, namely from the sense of power abstracted
" from the sense of good; and it is the same principle that
" makes us read with admiration and reconciles us in fact
" to the triumphant progress of the conquerors and mighty
" Hunters of mankind, who come to stop the Shepherd's
" Pipe upon the Mountains and sweep away his listening
" flock. Do you mean to deny that there is anything im-
" posing to the imagination in power, in grandeur, in out-
" ward show, in the accumulation of individual wealth and
" luxury, at the expense of equal justice and the common
" weal? Do you deny that there is anything in the 'Pride
" 'Pomp, and Circumstance of glorious war, that makes
" 'ambition virtue'? in the eyes of admiring multitudes?
" Is this a new theory of the pleasures of the imagination,
" which says that the pleasures of the imagination do not
" take rise so[le]ly in the calculation of the understanding?
" is it a paradox of my creating that 'one murder makes
" 'a villain, millions a Hero'! or is it not true, that here as
" in other cases, the enormity of the evil overpowers and
" makes a convert of the imagination by its very magni-
" tude? You contradict my reasoning because you know
" nothing of the question, and you think that no one has a
" right to understand what you do not. My offence against
" purity in the passage alluded to 'which contains the con-
" 'centrated venom of my malignity' is that I have admitted
" that there are tyrants and slaves abroad in the world;
" and you would hush the matter up and pretend that
" there is no such thing in order that there may be nothing
" else. Farther I have explained the cause, the subtle
" sophistry of the human mind, that tolerates and pampers
" the evil in order to guard against its approaches; you
" would conceal the cause in order to prevent the cure and

" to leave the proud flesh about the heart to harden and
" ossify into one impenetrable mass of selfishness and
" hypocrisy, that we may not 'sympathise in the distresses
" ' of suffering virtue' in any case in which they come in
" competition with the fictitious wants and 'imputed weak-
" ' nesses of the great.' You ask ' are we gratified by the
" ' cruelties of Domitian or Nero ?' No not we—they were
" too petty and cowardly to strike the imagination at a
" distance; but the Roman senate tolerated them, ad-
" dressed their perpetrators, exalted them into gods, the
" fathers of the people, they had pimps and scribblers of
" all sorts in their pay, their Senecas, &c., till a turbulent
" rabble thinking there were no injuries to Society greater
" than the endurance of unlimited and wanton oppression,
" put an end to the farce and abated the nuisance as well as
" they could. Had you and I lived in those times we should
" have been what we are now, I 'a sour mal content,' and
" you 'a sweet courtier.'" The manner in which this is
managed: the force and innate power with which it
yeasts and works up itself—the feeling for the costume
of society ; is in a style of genius. He hath a demon, as
he himself says of Lord Byron. We are to have a party
this evening. The Davenports from Church row—I dont
think you know anything of them—they have paid me a
good deal of attention. I like Davenport himself. The
names of the rest are Miss Barnes, Miss Winter with the
Children.

*At this point there is a break in the manuscript arising
from the fact that Keats overlooked a sheet when he de-
spatched the budget to his brother and sister-in-law. Fortu-
nately, however, some sort of transcript was made by Mr.
Jeffrey, and from that the missing passage can be tolerably
well restored. Keats eventually discovered his omission,*

and sent the omitted sheet on with another batch, having first added an explanatory paragraph under a new date as will be seen later on.

The words " Augustan Age of the Drama" in the seventh line of page 278, should be followed by "'Comme on sait' as Voltaire says"; and in the thirteenth line of the same page, the word " Bellamira" should be followed by " alias—(Alias—Yea and I say unto you a greater than Elias—there was Abbot, and talking of Abbot his name puts me in mind of a spelling book lesson, descriptive of the whole Dramatis personae—Abbot—Abbess—Actor—Actress—)".

The paragraph which ends with the second line on page 279 requires completion thus :

she is a make-believe—(she is bona *side* a thin young 'oman—). But this is mere talk of a fellow creature; yet pardie I would not that Henry have her. (Non volo ut eam possideat, nam, for, it would be a bam, for it would be a sham—). Don't think I am writing a petition to the Governors of St. Luke—no, that would be in another style. May it please your worships; forasmuch as the undersigned has committed, transferred, given up, made over, consigned, and aberrated himself, to the art and mystery of poetry; forasmuch as he hath cut, rebuffed affronted, huffed, and shirked, and taken stint, at all other employments, arts mysteries and occupations, honest, middling, and dishonest; forasmuch as he hath at sundry times and in diverse places, told truth unto the men of this generation, and eke to the women; moreover, forasmuch as he hath kept a pair of boots that did not fit, and doth not admire Sheild's [*sic*] play, Leigh Hunt, Tom Moore, Bob Southey and Mr. Rogers; and does admire Wm Hazlitt; more over[er] for as more as he liketh half of Wordsworth, and none of Crabbe; more over-est for for as most; as he hath written this page of penmanship, he prayeth your worships to give him a lodging—witnessed by Rd. Abbey and Co. cum familiaribus & consanguiniis (signed) Count de Cockaigne—

On the same page the paragraph ending with the word "perquisite" should be extended thus:

Parsons will always keep up their character, but as it is said there are some animals the ancients knew which we do not, let us hope our posterity will miss the black badger with tri-cornered hat; who knows but some Reviewer of Buffon or Pliny may put an account of the parson in the Appendix; No one will then believe it any more than we believe in the Phoenix. I think we may class the lawyer in the same natural history of monsters; a green bag will hold as much as a lawn sleeve. The only difference is that one is fustian and the other flimsy; I am not unwilling to read Church history—at present I have Milnes in my eye—his is reckoned a very good one.

18th September [1819]. In looking over some of my papers I found the above specimen of my carelessness. It is a sheet you ought to have had long ago—my letter must have appeared very unconnected, but as I number the sheets you must have discovered how the mistake happened. How many things have happened since I wrote it. How have I acted contrary to my resolves; the interval between writing this sheet and the day I put this supplement to it, has been completely filled with generous and most friendly actions of Brown towards me. How frequently I forget to speak of things which I think of and feel most. 'Tis very singular the idea about Buffon above, has been taken up by Hunt in the Examiner, in some papers which he calls "A Preternatural History."

After this point the holograph recommences, and shows again curious variations from the Jeffrey-Houghton version. In line 16 of page 280 "power" should be substituted for "frown"; and three lines lower down, where Poetry, Ambition and Love are described as three figures, the unwarrantable liberty has been taken of changing Keats's words from "a Man and two women" to "two men and a woman." After the allusion to the impending death of Haslam's father, in the next paragraph, editorial propriety has removed the harmless statement "his mother bears up, he says, very well." In the sixth line of page 281 the word "interested" should be "influenced"; and a few lines further on the sentence ending "injuring society" requires completion by the words—"which it would do I fear pushed to an extremity."

Before the sentence beginning "The noble animal Man" should be restored the words "they get their food in the same manner;" and on the next page (282) the passage about Socrates and Jesus has been so mis-handled that I give it from the holograph, after the words "Their histories evince it":

What I heard a little time ago, Taylor observe with respect to Socrates, may be said of Jesus—That he was so great a man that though he transmitted no writing of his own to posterity, we have his Mind and his sayings and his greatness handed to us by others. It is to be lamented that the history of the latter was written and revised by Men interested in the pious frauds of Religion. Yet through all this I see his splendour.

The new paragraph headed "15th April [1819]" at page 283 should open with "This is the 15th of April [1819]"; and between the words "write in the light" and "It looks so much like rain," the holograph contains the following mass of prose and a quantity of verse:

I was in town yesterday and at Taylor's heard that young Birkbeck had been in Town and was to set forward in six or seven days—so I shall dedicate that time to making up this parcel ready for him. I wish I could hear from you to make me "whole and general as the casing air." A few days after the 19th of April[1] I received a note from Haslam containing the news of his father's death. The Family has all been well. Haslam has his father's situation. The Framptons have behaved well to him. The day before yesterday I went to a rout at Sawrey's—it was made pleasant by Reynolds being there and our getting into conversation with one of the most beautiful Girls I ever saw. She gave a remarkable prettiness to all those commonplaces which most women who talk must utter. I like Mrs. Sawrey very well. The Sunday before last your Brothers were to come by a long invitation—so long that for the time I forgot it when I promised Mrs. Brawne to dine with her on the same day. On recollecting my engagement with your Brothers I immediately excused myself with Mrs. Brawne but she would not hear of it and insisted on my bringing my friends with me. So we all dined at Mrs. Brawne's. I have been to Mrs. Bentley's this morning and put all the letters to and from you and poor

---

[1] Keats of course meant the 19th of March: it was only the 15th of April when he was writing.

Tom and me [*sic*]. I found some of the correspondence between him and that degraded Wells and Amena. It is a wretched business, I do not know the rights of it—but what I do know would I am sure affect you so much that I am in two Minds whether I will tell you anything about it. And yet I do not see why—for anything tho' it be unpleasant that calls to mind those we still love has a compensation in itself for the pain it occasions—so very likely tomorrow I may set about copying the whole of what I have about it: with no sort of a Richardson selfsatisfaction—I hate it to a sickness—and I am afraid more from indolence of mind than anything else. I wonder how people exist with all their worries. I have not been to Westminster but once lately and that was to see Dilke in his new Lodgings—I think of living somewhere in the neighbourhood myself. Your mother was well by your Brothers' account. I shall see her perhaps tomorrow—yes I shall. We have had the Boys here lately—they make a bit of a racket—I shall not be sorry when they go. I found also this morning in a note from George to you my dear sister a lock of your hair which I shall this moment put in the miniature case. A few days ago Hunt dined here and Brown invited Davenport to meet him. Davenport from a sense of weakness thought it incumbent on him to show off—and pursuant to that never ceased talking and boaring [*sic*] all day till I was completely fagged out—Brown grew melancholy—but Hunt perceiving what a complimentary tendency all this had bore it remarkably well—Brown grumbled about it for two or three days. I went with Hunt to Sir John Leicester's gallery; there I saw Northcote—Hilton—Bewick and many more of great and Little note. Haydon's picture is of very little progress this year. He talks about finishing it next year.

Wordsworth is going to publish a Poem called Peter Bell —what a perverse fellow it is! Why will he talk about Peter Bells—I was told not to tell—but to you it will not be telling—Reynolds hearing that said Peter Bell was coming out, took it into his head to write a skit upon it called Peter Bell. He did it as soon as thought on; it is to be published this morning, and comes out before the real Peter Bell, with this admirable motto from the "Bold stroke for a Wife" "I am the real Simon Pure." It would be just as well to trounce Lord Byron in the same manner.[1] I am still at a stand in versifying—I cannot do it yet with any pleasure—I mean however to look round on my resources and means —and see what I can do without poetry. To that end I shall live in Westminster. I have no doubt of making by some means a little to help on or I shall be left in the Lurch—with the burden of a little Pride. However I look in time. The Dilkes like their Lodgings at Westminster tolerably well. I cannot help thinking what a shame it is that poor Dilke should give up his comfortable house and garden for his Son, whom he will certainly ruin with too much care. The boy has nothing in his ears all day but himself and the importance of his

---

[1] This juxtaposition of the names of Byron and Wordsworth in such a context tempts one to recall an epigram by another poet who shared Keats's opinion that those two luminaries were not altogether free from reproach. Landor, in his *Dry Sticks*, has the following lines "To Recruits"—

> Ye who are belted and alert to go
> Where bays, won only in hard battles, grow,
> Asthmatic Wordsworth, Byron piping-hot,
> Leave in the rear, and march with manly Scott.
> Along the coast prevail malignant heats,
> Halt on high ground behind the shade of Keats.

education. Dilke has continually in his mouth "My Boy." This is what spoils princes: it may have the same effect with Commoners. Mrs. Dilke has been very well lately. But what a shameful thing it is that for that obstinate Boy Dilke should stifle himself in Town Lodgings and wear out his Life by his continual apprehension of his Boy's fate in Westminster school with the rest of the Boys and the Masters. Every one has some wear and tear. One would think Dilke ought to be quiet and happy—but no—this one Boy makes his face pale, his society silent and his vigilance jealous. He would I have no doubt quarrel with anyone who snubb'd his Boy. With all this he has no notion how to manage him. O what a farce is our greatest cares! Yet one must be in the pother for the sake of Clothes food and Lodging. There has been a squabble between Kean and Mr. Bucke. There are faults on both sides—on Bucke's the faults are positive to the Question: Kean's fault is a want of genteel knowledge and high Policy. The former writes knavishly foolish and the other silly bombast. It was about a Tragedy written by said Mr. Bucke which it appears Mr. Kean kick'd at—it was so bad. After a little struggle of Mr. Bucke's against Kean drury Lane had the Policy to bring it out and Kean the impolicy not to appear in it. It was damn'd. The people in the Pit had a favourite call on the night of "Buck Buck rise up" and "Buck Buck how many horns do I hold up." Kotzebue the German Dramatist and traitor to his country was murdered lately by a young student whose name I forget—he stabbed himself immediately after crying out "Germany! Germany!" I was unfortunate to miss Richards the only time I have been for many months to see him. Shall I treat you with a little extempore?—

Here follow the ninety-six lines of verse which will be found among the fresh poetry and new readings (see pages 31 to 34 of this volume). Keats then breaks off his extempore, as suddenly as he had begun it, with the following:—

Brown is gone to bed—and I am tired of rhyming—there is a north wind blowing playing young gooseberry with the trees. I don't care so it helps even with a side wind a Letter to me—for I cannot put faith in any reports I hear of the Settlement some are good and some bad. Last Sunday I took a walk towards Highgate and in the lane that winds by the side of Lord Mansfield's park I met Mr. Green our Demonstrator at Guy's in conversation with Coleridge. I joined them after enquiring by a look whether it would be agreeable. I walked with him a[t] his alderman-after-dinner pace for near two miles I suppose. In those two miles he broached a thousand things—let me see if I can give you a list—Nightingales, Poetry—on Poetical Sensation—Metaphysics—Different genera and species of Dreams—Nightmare—a dream accompanied with a sense of touch—single and double touch—a dream related—First and second consciousness—the difference explained between will and Volition—so m[an]y metaphysicians from a want of smoking the second consciousness—Monsters—the Kraken—Mermaids—Southey believes in them—Southey's belief too much diluted—a Ghost story—Good morning—I heard his voice as he came towards me—I heard it as he moved away—I had heard it all the interval—if it may be called so. He was civil enough to ask me to call on him at Highgate. Good night!

It will be seen that the few lines about Brown's having gone to bed, embodied in the foregoing passage, had been garbled and misplaced in the version reprinted at the top of page 284. In place of the three lines and a half following "patient Griselda" the original letter has the following:

The servant has come for the little Browns this morning—they have been a toothache to me which I shall enjoy the riddance of. Their little voices are like wasps' stings. Sometimes am I all wound with Browns.[1] We had a claret feast some little while ago. There were Dilke, Reynolds, Skinner, Mancur, John Brown, Martin, Brown and I. We all got a little tipsy—but pleasantly so. I enjoy Claret to a degree. I have been looking over the correspondence of the pretended Amena and Wells this evening. I now see the whole cruel deception. I think Wells must have had an accomplice in it. Amena's Letters are in a Man's language and in a Man's hand imitating a woman's. The instigations to this diabolical scheme were vanity and the love of intrigue. It was no thoughtless hoax—but a cruel deception on a sanguine Temperament, with every show of friendship. I do not think death too bad for the villain. The world would look upon it in a different light should I expose it—they would call it a frolic—so I must be wary—but I consider it my duty to be prudently revengeful. I will hang over his head like a sword by a hair. I will be opium to his vanity if I cannot injure his interests. He is a rat and he shall have ratsbane to his vanity. I will harm him all I possibly can. I have no doubt I shall be able to do so. Let us leave him to his misery alone except when we can throw in a little more.

At page 285, in line 3, "bever" should replace "bite"; and between "always with my Compliments" and "After you have eaten your breakfast," should be inserted—

---

[1] Compare *The Tempest*, Act II, Scene II:
        sometime am I
All wound with Adders.

When you are both set down to breakfast I advise you to eat your full share—but leave off immediately on feeling yourself inclined to anything on the other side of the puffy—avoid that for it does not become young women.

The words printed at the top of page 286 as " tear off his buttons" should, it seems, be "Sew off his buttons"; they should follow a full stop, and be followed by this passage:—

Yesterday I could not write a line I was so fatigued for the day before I went to town in the morning called on your Mother, and returned in time for a few friends we had to dinner. These were Taylor, Woodhouse, Reynolds—we began cards at about 9 o'Clock, and the night coming on and continuing dark and rainy they could not think of returning to town. So we played at Cards till very daylight—and yesterday I was not worth a sixpence. Your Mother was very well but anxious for a Letter. We had half an hour talk and no more for I was obliged to be home. Mrs. and Miss Millar were well and so was Miss Waldegrave. I have asked your Brothers here for next Sunday. When Reynolds was here on Monday—he asked me to give Hunt a hint to take notice of his Peter Bell in the Examiner—the best thing I can do is to write a little notice of it myself which I will do here and copy out if it should suit my Purpose. "*Peter Bell.* There have been lately advertized two Books both Peter Bell by name; what stuff the one was made of might be seen by the motto 'I am the real Simon Pure.' This false florimel has hurried from the press and obtruded herself into public notice while for ought we know the real one may be still wandering about the woods and mountains. Let us hope she may soon make her appearance and make good her right to the magic girdle. The Pamphleteering Archimage we can perceive has rather a splenetic love than a downright hatred to real florimels—if indeed they had been so christened—or had even a pretention to play at bob cherry with Barbara Lewthwaite: but he has a fixed aversion to those three rhyming Graces Alice Fell, Susan Gale and Betty Foy ~~and who can wonder at it?~~ and now at length especially to Peter Bell—fit Apollo. ~~The writer of this little skit from understanding~~ It may be seen from one or two Passages of in this little skit, that the writer of it has felt the finer parts of Mr. Wordsworths ~~Poetry,~~ and perhaps expatiated with his more remote and sublimer muse; ~~who sits aloof in a cheerful sadness, and~~ This as far as it relates to Peter Bell is unlucky. The more he may love the sad embroidery of the Excursion; the more he will hate the coarse Samplers of Betty Foy and Alice Fell; and as they come from the same hand, the better will be able to imitate that which can be imitated, to wit Peter Bell—as far as can be imagined from the obstinate name. We repeat it is very unlucky—this real Simon Pure is in parts the very Man—there is a pernicious likeness in the scenery, a 'pestilent humour' in the rhymes and an inveterate cadence in some of the Stanzas that must be lamented. If we are one part ~~pleased~~ amused with this we are three parts sorry that an appreciator of Wordsworth should show so much temper at this really provoking name of Peter Bell—!" This will do well enough—I have copied it and enclosed it to Hunt. You will call it a little politic—seeing I keep clear of all parties—I say something for and against both parties—and suit it to the tune of the Examiner—I meant to say I do not unsuit it—and I believe I think what I say—nay I am sure I do—I and my conscience are in luck to day —which is an excellent thing. The other night I went to the Play with Rice, Reynolds and Martin—we saw a new dull and half damn'd opera call'd "the Heart of Mid Lothian"—that was on Saturday. I stopt at Taylor's on Sunday with Woodhouse—and passed a quiet sort of pleasant day. I have been very much pleased with the Panorama of the Ships at the north Pole—with the icebergs, the Mountains, the Bears, the Wolves—the seals, the Penguins—and a large whale floating back above water—it is impossible to describe the place.

Wednesday Evening—
La belle dame sans merci—

The little review of "Peter Bell" was printed in "The Examiner" for April 25, 1819, with some modification (see page 48 of this volume). The heading given above is followed in the holograph by the wonderful ballad of "La Belle Dame," showing revisions of text of the most interesting kind. At the close of the poem is the following charming comment:

Why four kisses—you will say—why four because I wish to restrain the headlong impetuosity of my Muse—she would have fain said "score" without hurting the rhyme—but we must temper the Imagination as the Critics say with Judgment. I was obliged to choose an even number that both eyes might have fair play, and to speak truly I think two a piece quite sufficient. Suppose I had said seven there would have been three and a half a piece—a very awkward affair and well got out of on my side—

This immediately precedes the " Chorus of Fairies 4 Fire, air, earth and water—Salamander, Zephyr, Dusketha, Breama—" which will be found at pages 340 to 344 of Volume II; and that poem is followed by an unusually thoughtful passage of prose, to wit—

I have been reading lately two very different books,

Robertson's America and Voltaire's Siecle de Louis xiv. It is like walking arm and arm between Pizarro and the great-little Monarch. In how lamentable a case do we see the great body of the people in both instances; in the first when Men might seem to inherit quiet of Mind from unsophisticated senses; from uncontamination of civilization and especially from their being as it were estranged from the mutual helps of Society and its mutual injuries—and thereby more immediately under the Protection of Providence—even there they had mortal pains to bear as bad, or even worse than Ba[i]liffs, Debts and Poverties of civilized Life. The whole appears to resolve into this—that Man is originally a poor forked creature subject to the same mischances as the beasts of the forest, destined to hardships and disquietude of some kind or other. If he improves by degrees his bodily accom[m]odations and comforts—at each stage, at each accent there are waiting for him a fresh set of annoyances—he is mortal and there is still a heaven with its stars above his head. The most interesting question that can come before us is, How far by the persevering endeavours of a seldom appearing Socrates Mankind may be made happy—I can imagine such happiness carried to an extreme—but what must it end in?—Death—and who could in such a case bear with death—the whole troubles of life which are now frittered away in a series of years, would the[n] be accumulated for the last days of a being who instead of hailing its approach would leave this world as Eve left Paradise. But in truth I do not at all believe in this sort of perfectibility—the nature of the world will not admit of it—the inhabitants of the world will correspond to itself. Let the fish Philosophise the ice away from the Rivers in winter time and they shall be at continual play in the tepid delight of summer. Look at the

Poles and at the Sands of Africa, whirlpools and volcanoes. Let men exterminate them and I will say that they may arrive at earthly Happiness. The point at which Man may arrive is as far as the para[l]lel state in inanimate nature and no further. For instance suppose a rose to have sensation, it blooms on a beautiful morning, it enjoys itself, but then comes a cold wind, a hot sun—it cannot escape it, it cannot destroy its annoyances—they are as native to the world as itself—no more can man be happy in spite, the worldly elements will prey upon his nature. The common cognomen of this world among the misguided and superstitious is "a vale of tears" from which we are to be redeemed by a certain arbitrary interposition of God and taken to Heaven. What a little circumscribed straightened [*sic*] notion! Call the world if you please "The vale of Soul-making." Then you will find out the use of the world (I am speaking now in the highest terms for human nature admitting it to be immortal which I will here take for granted for the purpose of showing a thought which has struck me concerning it) I say "*Soul making*"—Soul as distinguished from an Intelligence. There may be intelligences or sparks of the divinity in millions—but they are not Souls till they acquire identities, till each one is personally itself. Intelligences are atoms of perception —they know and they see and they are pure, in short they are God.—How then are Souls to be made? How then are these sparks which are God to have identity given them—so as ever to possess a bliss peculiar to each one's individual existence? How but by the medium of a world like this? This point I sincerely wish to consider because I think it a grander system of salvation than the christian religion—or rather it is a system of spirit creation. This is effected by three grand materials acting the one upon the other for a series of years. These three materials are the *Intelligence* the *human heart* (as distinguished from intelligence or Mind) and the *World* or *Elemental space* suited for the proper action of *Mind and Heart* on each other for the purpose of forming the *Soul* or *Intelligence destined to possess the sense of Identity*. I can scarcely express what I but dimly perceive—and yet I think I perceive it—that you may judge the more clearly I will put it in the most homely form possible. I will call the *world* a School instituted for the purpose of teaching little children to read—I will call the *human heart* the *horn Book* read in that School—and I will call the *Child able to read the Soul* made from that *School* and its *horn book*. Do you not see how necessary a World of Pains and troubles is to school an Intelligence and make it a Soul? A Place where the heart must feel and suffer in a thousand diverse ways. Not merely is the Heart a Hornbook, It is the Mind's Bible, it is the Mind's experience, it is the text from which the Mind or Intelligence sucks its identity. As various as the Lives of Men are—so various become their Souls, and thus does God make individual beings, Souls, Identical Souls of the sparks of his own essence. This appears to me a faint sketch of a system of Salvation which does not offend our reason and humanity. I am convinced that many difficulties which christians labour under would vanish before it—there is one which even now strikes me—the salvation of Children. In them the spark or intelligence returns to God without any identity —it having had no time to learn of and be altered by the heart—or seat of the human Passions. It is pretty generally suspected that the christian scheme has been copied from the ancient Persian and Greek Philosophers. Why may they not have made this simple thing even more simple for common apprehension by introducing Mediators and Personages in the same manner as in the he[a]then mythology abstractions are personified? Seriously I think it probable that this system of Soul-making—may have been the Parent of all the more palpable and personal schemes of Redemption among the Zoroastrians, the Christians and the Hindoos. For as one part of the human species must have their carved Jupiter; so another part must have the palpable and named Mediation and Saviour, their Christ, their Oromanes and their Vishnu. If what I have said should not be plain enough, as I fear it may not be, I will put you in the place where I began in this series of thoughts—I mean I began by seeing how man was formed by circumstances—and what are circumstances? but touchstones of his heart? and what are touchstones but provings of his heart, but fortifiers or alterers of his nature? and what is his altered nature but his Soul?—and what was his Soul before it came into the world and had these provings and alterations and perfectionings?—An intelligence without Identity—and how is this Identity to be made? Through the medium of the Heart? and how is the heart to become this Medium but in a world of Circumstances? There now I think what with Poetry and Theology you may thank your stars that my pen is not very long winded. Yesterday I received two Letters from your Mother and Henry which I shall send by young Birkbeck with this.

Friday April 30th—Brown has been here rummaging up some of my old sins—that is to say sonnets. I do not think you remember them so I will copy them out as well as two or three lately written. I have just written one on Fame which Brown is transcribing and he has his book and mine. I must employ myself perhaps in a sonnet on the same subject.

For the two sonnets on Fame and one to Sleep, which follow in the holograph, see Volume II, pages 345 to 348. The letter proceeds as at page 286 of the third volume, with the paragraph beginning "The following poem" and the Ode to Psyche; and after that poem are the words

> Here endethe ye Ode to Psyche.
> Incipit altera Sonneta.

I have been endeavouring &c. (*as at page 286, with slight verbal variation*).

The following new letter of the Winchester series should be read between Letters CVII and CVIII, pages 324 and 325 of Volume III.

Winchester Sept 1. 1819.

My dear Taylor

Brown and I have been employed for these 3 weeks past from time to time in writing to our different friends—a dead silence is our only answer—no mail morning after morning. Tuesday is the day for the Examiner to arrive, this is the 2^d Tuesday which has been barren even of a Newspaper—Men should be in imitation of Spirits "responsive to each others note". Instead of that I pipe and no one hath danced. We have been cursing like Mandeville and Lisle. With this I shall send by the same post a 3^d letter to a friend of mine who though it is of consequence has neither answered right or left. We have been much in want of news from the Theatres having heard that Kean is going to America—but no—not a word. Why I should come on you with all these complaints I cannot explain to myself, especially as I suspect you must be in the country. Do answer me soon for I really must know something. I must steer myself by the rudder of Information.

ever yours sincerely
John Keats.

In reprinting the great Winchester journal-letter begun on Friday the 17th of September 1819 (see Volume IV, pages 3 to 34), Mr. Speed reproduces most of the old mistakes of the version published in the New York " World," and introduces a few fresh ones, as well as several new passages, and a foot-note which is interesting if trustworthy. Adverting to Keats's statement that he " cannot help thinking Mr. Audubon a dishonest man," Mr. Speed says " Audubon, the naturalist, sold to George Keats a boat loaded with merchandise, which at the time of the sale Audubon knew to be at the bottom of the Mississippi River." The first new passage is in that part of the letter where the poet tells of his return to Winchester after posting to Town on George's business, after the words " they must be," line 6, page 6. In the " World " version (followed in this respect in the body of the library edition) this is disposed of by the first 13 words of the following paragraph; and a full-stop is placed after " alone," without mark of omission :—

I returned to Winchester the day before yesterday, and am now here alone, for Brown some days before I left, went to Bedhampton, and there he will be for the next fortnight. The term of his house [1] will be up in the middle of next month, when we shall return to Hamp-

---

[1] It is perhaps worth while to explain that Brown was in the habit of letting his house in Wentworth Place, where he and Keats domesticated together, and that he generally arranged to go off on country trips during those terms for which the house was thus profitably employed.

stead. On Sunday I dined with your mother and Hen and Charles in Henrietta Street. Mrs. and Miss Millar were in the country. Charles had been but a few days returned from Paris. I dare say you will have letters expressing the motives of his journey. Mrs. Wylie and Miss Waldegrave seem as quiet as two mice there alone. I did not show your last. I thought it better not, for better times will certainly come, and why should they be unhappy in the meantime?

The next interpolation of the American editor in the Winchester journal-letter is before the words " When I left Mr. Abbey," Volume IV, page 11, *line* 12 : *the fresh passage reads thus, or rather, I presume, should read thus ; for Mr. Speed does not give the extract from Burton :—*

I have been reading lately Burton's "Anatomy of Melancholy," and I think you will be very much amused with a page I here copy for you. I call it a Feu de Joie round the batteries of Fort St. Hyphen-de-Phrase on the birthday of the Digamma. The whole alphabet was drawn up in a phalanx on the corner of an old dictionary, band playing "Amo, amas, &c."

" Every lover admires his mistress, though she be very
" deformed of her self, ill-favored, wrinkled, pimpled, pale,
" red, yellow, tan'd, tallow-faced, have a swoln juglers
" platter face, or a thin, lean, chitty face, have clouds in her
" face, be crooked, dry, bald, goggle-ey'd, blear-ey'd or
" with staring eys, she looks like a squis'd cat, hold her
" head still awry, heavy, dull, hollow-ey'd, black or yellow
" about the eys, or squint-ey'd, sparrow-mouthed, Persean
" hook-nosed, have a sharp fox nose, a red nose, China
" flat, great nose, *nare simo patuloque*, a nose like a pro-
" montory, gubber-tushed, rotten teeth, black, uneven,
" brown teeth, beetle browed, a witches beard, her breath

"stink all over the room, her nose drop winter and summer,
"with a Bavarian poke under her chin, a sharp chin, lave
"eared, with a long cranes neck, which stands awry too,
"*pendulis mammis, her dugs like two double jugs*, or else
"no dugs in the other extream, bloody faln-fingers, she
"have filthy long unpaired nails, scabbed hands or wrists,
"a tan'd skin, a rotten carcass, crooked back, she stoops,
"is lame, splea-footed, *as slender in the middle as a
"cow in the wast*, gowty legs, her ankles hang over her
"shooes, her feet stink, she breed lice, a meer change-
"ling, a very monster, an aufe imperfect, her whole com-
"plexion savours, an harsh voyce, incondite gesture, vile
"gate, a vast virago, or an ugly·tit, a slug, a fat fusti-
"lugs, a trusse, a long lean rawbone, a skeleton, a
"sneaker (*si qua latent meliora puta*), and to thy judg-
"ment looks like a mard in a lanthorn, whom thou
"couldst not fancy for a world, but hatest, loathest, and
"wouldst have spit in her face, or blow thy nose in her
"bosome, *remedium amoris* to another man, a dowdy, a
"slut, a scold, a nasty, rank, rammy, filthy, beastly quean,
"dishonest peradventure, obscene, base, beggerly, rude,
"foolish, untaught, peevish, Irus daughter, Thersites sister,
"Grobians scholler; if he love her once, he admires her
"for all this, he takes no notice of any such errours, or
"imperfections of body or mind."[1]

There's a dose for you. Fire!! I would give my favourite leg to have written this as a speech in a play.

---

[1] I am in some doubt whether Keats took the trouble to write out more or less than I have given of Burton's strange out-pouring of ugly phrases. Mr. Speed says "Here follows a page taken from Part III. Sec. 2, on the Symptoms of Love,—' Every lover admires his mistress,' etc. etc." But whether a page of Keats's letter, or a page of Burton's book, and if so of what edition, we are left to guess.

With what effect could Matthews popgun it at the pit! This, I think, will amuse you more than so much poetry. Of that I do not like to copy any, as I am afraid it is too *mal à propos* for you at present; and yet I will send you some, for by the time you receive it, things in England may have taken a different turn.

The next point in the Winchester letter at which we get some interesting variations from the "World" version is where Keats inserts his old Derrynaculen letter. After the words "Incipit epistola caledoniensa" (Volume IV, page 15) we have now the characteristic confession of dependence on Brown for any chance knowledge of the lapse of time on the Scotch tour:—

I did not know the day of the month, for I find I have not added it. Brown must have been asleep.

And then before he proceeds to copy the letter varying so curiously from the almost identical one which he wrote to Thomas Keats on the 23rd of July 1818, he gives the following parenthetical explanation of his reasons for copying it instead of enclosing it:—

(before I go any further, I must premise that I would send the identical letter, instead of taking the trouble to copy it; I do not do so, for it would spoil my notion of the neat manner in which I intend to fold these three genteel sheets. The original is written on coarse paper,[1] and the soft ones would ride in the post-bag very uneasy. Perhaps there might be a quarrel).

---

[1] If there were any doubt as to the genuineness of the Winchester letter or the new additions to it, here were a point of vantage. It is an undoubted fact that the Scotch letters were on "coarse paper": most of those I have seen are on folio sheets of thick foolscap.

Next, in that part of the Winchester letter describing the election of the Mayor—or rather the need there was before that event that some excitement should supervene upon the remarkable sleepiness of the place, there is the following interpolation after the words " they have not exposed themselves in the street" (Volume IV, page 18, *last line*) :—

The first night, tho', of our arrival here there was a slight uproar took place at about ten of the clock. We heard distinctly a noise patting down the street, as of a walking-cane of the good old dowager breed; and a little minute after we heard a less voice observe, "What a noise the ferril made—it must be loose." Brown wanted to call the constables, but I observed it was only a little breeze, and would soon pass over.[1]

In the same letter, after the mention of certain specks on the teeth of the servant who admitted Keats at Mrs. Wylie's (Volume IV, page 22), *Mr. Speed gives the following passage* :—

Your mother said something about Miss Keasle—what that was is quite a riddle to me now, whether she had got fatter or thinner, or broader or longer, straiter, or had taken to the zigzags—whether she had taken to or left off asses' milk. That, by the by, she ought never to touch. How much better it would be to put her out to nurse with the wise woman of Brentford. I can say no more on so spare a subject. Miss Millar, now, is a different morsel, if one knew how to divide and subdivide, theme her out into sections and subsections, lay a little on every part of her body as it is divided in common with all her fellow-creatures, in Moor's Almanack. But,

---

[1] The same passage, it seems, needs restoration to the same context in the letter to Reynolds, No. CIX, Volume III, page 328.

alas, I have not heard a word about her, no cue to begin upon: there was indeed a buzz about her and her mother's being at old Mrs. So and So's, *who was like to die*, as the Jews say. But I daresay, keeping up their dialect, *she was not like to die.*

After the warning words " But be careful of those Americans" (Volume IV, page 30), *Mr. Speed has the following passage in place of and including the few lines given before :—*

I could almost advise you to come when ever you have the sum of £500 to England. Those Americans will, I am afraid, still fleece you. If ever you think of such a thing, you must bear in mind the very different state of society here,—the immense difficulties of the times, the great sum required per annum to maintain yourself in any decency. In fact, the whole is with Providence. I know not how to advise you but by advising you to advise with yourself. In your next tell me at large your thoughts about America,—what chance there is of succeeding there, for it appears to me you have as yet been somehow deceived. I cannot help thinking Mr. Audubon has deceived you. I shall not like the sight of him. I shall endeavour to avoid seeing him. You see how puzzled I am. I have no meridian to fix you to, being the slave of what is to happen. I think I may bid you, finally, remain in good hopes, and not tease yourself with my changes and variations of mind. If I say nothing decisive in any one particular part of my letter, you may glean the truth from the whole pretty correctly. You may wonder why I had not put your affairs with Abbey in train on receiving your letter before last, to which there will reach you a short answer dated from Shanklin. I did write and speak to Abbey, but to no purpose. Your last, with the enclosed note, has appealed home to him. He will not see the necessity of a thing till he is hit in the mouth. 'Twill be effectual. I am sorry to mix up foolish and serious things together, but in writing so much I am obliged to do so, and I hope sincerely the tenor of your mind will maintain itself better.

Coming to the latter portion of the Winchester letter, the portion addressed particularly to Mrs. George Keats, we find the following sentences given by Mr. Speed next to the words " No step hasty or injurious to you must be taken" (Volume IV, page 33, line 6) :—

You say let one large sheet be all to me. You will find more than that in different parts of this packet for you. Certainly, I have been caught in rains. A catch in the rain occasioned my last sore throat; but as for red-haired girls, upon my word, I do not recollect ever having seen one. Are you quizzing me or Miss Waldegrave when you talk of promenading?

The short conclusion of the letter (same page), in which George is again directly addressed, is more than doubled in extent in the new version,—the following passage having been inserted after the assurance " You shall not have cause to think I neglect you" :—

I have kept this back a little time in expectation of hearing from Mr. Abbey. You will say I might have remained in town to be Abbey's messenger in these affairs. That I offered him, but he in his answer convinced me he was anxious to bring the business to an issue. He observed, that by being himself the agent in the whole, people might be more expeditious. You say you have not heard for three months, and yet your letters have the tone of knowing how our affairs are situated, by which I conjecture I acquainted you with them in a letter previous to the Shanklin one. That I may not have done. To be certain I will here state that it is in consequence of Mr. Jennings[1] threatening a chancery suit that you have been kept from the receipt of monies and myself deprived of any help from Abbey. I am glad you say you keep up your spirits. I hope you make a true statement on that score. Still keep them up, for we are all young. I can only repeat here that you shall hear from me again immediately. Notwithstanding this bad intelligence, I have experienced some pleasure in receiving so correctly two letters from you, as it gives me, if I may so say, a distant idea of proximity. This last improves upon my little niece—kiss her for me.

The next new letter is addressed to "Jas. Rice Esq., Poland St. Oxford [Street]" and seems to belong to December 1819.

Wentworth Place.

My dear Rice

As I want the coat on my back mended, I would be obliged if you would send me the one Brown left at your house by the Bearer—During your late contest I had regular reports of you, how that your time was completely taken up and your health improving—I shall call in the course of a few days, and see whether your promotion has made any difference in your Behaviour to us. I suppose Reynolds has given you an account of

---

[1] It is to be presumed that the *Mr.* Jennings of this passage has been evolved out of the inner consciousness of Mr. Speed; and that we should read *Mrs.* for *Mr.* The claim and threat in question were certainly on the part of Keats's *Aunt*; and I see no reason for supposing the aforementioned *Mr.* to be other than mythical.

Brown and Elliston. As he has not rejected our Tragedy, I shall not venture to call him directly a fool; But as he wishes to put it off till next season, I cannot help thinking him little better than a knave.—That it will not be acted this season is yet uncertain. Perhaps we may give it another furbish and try it at Covent Garden. 'Twould do one's heart good to see Macready in Ludolph. If you do not see me soon it will be from the humour of writing, which I have had for three days continuing. I must say to the Muses what the maid says to the man—" Take me while the fit is on me."— Would you like a true story? " There was a man and his wife who being to go a long Journey on foot, in the course of their travels came to a river which rolled knee-deep over the pebbles—In these cases the man generally pulls off his shoes and stockings, and carries the woman over on his back. This man did so. And his wife being pregnant and troubled, as in such cases is very common, with strange longings, took the strangest that ever was heard of. Seeing her husband's foot, a handsome one enough, look very clean and tempting in the clear water, on their arrival at the other bank, she earnestly demanded a bit of it. He being an affectionate fellow, and fearing for the comeliness of his child, gave her a bit which he cut off with his clasp knife.—Not satisfied, she asked for another morsel. Supposing there might be twins, he gave her a slice more. Not yet contented she craved another piece. 'You wretch,' cries the man, 'would you wish me to kill myself?—Take that'— upon which he stabbed her with the knife, cut her open, and found three children in her Belly: two of them very comfortable with their mouths shut, the third with its eyes and mouth stark staring wide open. ' Who would have thought it,' cried the Widower, and pursued his

Journey—". Brown has a little rumbling in his stomach this morning—

Ever yours sincerely,
John Keats.—

This letter is from the material gathered by Mr. Colvin, and is not, of course, to be found in Mr. Speed's book. The rest of the American editor's interpolations are in letter No. CXXIII of this edition, which will be found in Volume IV, at pages 50 to 57. Mr. Speed rejects as a forgery (!) the choicest passage in the letter as it stands in my edition, the passage recovered from " The Philobiblion" ; but what he interpolates, taken in conjunction with that passage, goes far to render the whole composition a masterpiece of letter-writing. Addressing his sister-in-law in a letter to be conveyed to her by his brother, Keats says, in a few lines which Mr. Speed has inserted after the words " in good health" (lines 3 and 4 of the letter) :—

To write to you by him is almost like following one's own letter in the mail. That it may not be quite so, I will leave common intelligence out of the question, and write wide of him as I can.

The following little bit of sober seriousness Mr. Speed places between the words " success of my friends" and " We smoke George about his little girl" (page 51) :—

I could almost promise that if I had the means I would accompany George back to America, and pay you a visit of a few months. I should not think much of the time, or my absence from my books; or I have no right to think, for I am very idle. But then I ought to be diligent, and at least keep myself within the reach of materials for diligence. Diligence, that I do not mean to say; I should say dreaming over my books, or rather other people's books. George has promised to bring you to England when the five years have elapsed. I regret very much that I shall not be able to see you before that time, and even then I must hope that your affairs will be in so prosperous a way as to induce you to stop longer. Yours is a hardish fate, to be so divided from your friends and settled among a people you hate. You will find it improve. You have a heart that will take hold of your children; even George's absence will make things better. His return will banish what must be your greatest sorrow, and at the same time minor ones with it. Robinson Crusoe,[1] when he saw himself in danger of perishing on the waters, looked back to his island as to the haven of his happiness, and on gaining it once more was more content with his solitude.

The following interpolated passage, belonging between the words "engraved in the middle of it" and "The evening before last," at page 52 of Volume IV, is useful as revealing the name of "Fool L" and showing that the mysterious "H" who made such a ridiculous lover (pages 7 and 8 of Volume IV) was almost of a certainty Haslam:—

Charles had a silk handkerchief belonging to a Miss

---

[1] Note the evidence of Keats's familiarity with De Foe's great work: since issuing this edition of Keats in 1883, a reperusal of *Robinson Crusoe* in the orthography of the first edition has convinced me that the book must be taken into account among the sources of Keats's English. There is great similarity of spelling, capitalling, inflexion, &c., between Keats's writings and the first edition of *Robinson Crusoe*; and this direct evidence of familiarity with the book is satisfactory.

Grover, with whom he pretended to be smitten, and for her sake kept exhibiting and adoring the handkerchief all the evening. Fool Lacon, Esqre., treated[1] it with a little venturesome, trembling contumely, whereon Charles set him quietly down on the floor,[2] from where he as quietly got up. This process was repeated at supper time, when your mother said, "If I were you, Mr. Lacon, I would not let him do so." Fool Lacon, Esqre., did not offer any remark. He will undoubtedly die in his bed. Your mother did not look quite so well on Sunday. Mrs. Henry Wylie is excessively quiet before people. I hope she is always so. Yesterday we dined at Taylor's, in Fleet street. George left early after dinner to go to Deptford; he will make all square there for me. I could not go with him—I did not like the amusement. Haslam is a very good fellow indeed; he has been excessively anxious and kind to us. But is this fair? He has an innamorata at Deptford, and he has been wanting me for some time past to see her. This is a thing which it is impossible not to shirk. A man is like a magnet—he must have a repelling end. So how am I to see Haslam's lady and family, if I even went? for by the time I got to Greenwich I should have repell'd them to Blackheath, and by the time I got to Deptford they would be on Shooters' Hill; when I came to Shooters' Hill they would alight at Chatham, and so on till I drove them into the sea, which I think might be indictable.

After the reference to the Scotchman at Taylor's who

---

[1] Presumably what Keats wrote was *treated*; but Mr. Speed prints *heated*.

[2] This phrase may be either literal or figurative. "To set a man down" is of course a common phrase enough; but "to set a man down on the floor" is certainly not a common form of the figure.

" was as clean as he could get himself" (Volume IV, page 52), we get in the American edition the following piece, which is all new save the reference to the introduction of Mr. Hart by George Keats; and even there the name is newly given in full :—

Not having succeeded in Drury Lane with our tragedy, we have been making some alterations, and are about to try Covent Garden. Brown has just done patching up the copy,—as it is altered. The reliance I had on it was in Kean's acting. I am not afraid it will be damn'd in the Garden. You said in one of your letters that there was nothing but Haydon & Co. in mine. There can be nothing of him in this, for I never see him or Co. George has introduced to us an American of the name of Hart. I like him in a moderate way. He was at Mrs. Dilke's party, and sitting by me; we began talking about English and American ladies. The Miss —— and some of their friends made not a very enticing row opposite us. I bade him mark them and form his judgement of them.

The passage about scandal and fun which, in this edition, ends with the word "ours" at the top of page 53, Volume IV, is succeeded in the American book by the following passage, which is all new except the opening sentence, that about Mrs. George Keats shooting, and a few words concerning her brothers :—

There were very good pickings for me in George's letters about the prairie settlement, if I had any taste to turn them to account in England. I knew a friend of Miss Andrews, yet I never mentioned her to him; for after I had read the letter I really did not recollect her story. Now I have been sitting here a half hour, with my invention at work, to say something about your mother or Charles or Henry, but it is in vain. I know not what to say. Three nights since, George went with your mother to the play. I hope she will soon see mine acted. I do not remember ever to have thanked you for your tassels to my Shakspeare—there he hangs so ably supported opposite me. I thank you now. It is a continual memento of you. If you should have a boy, do not christen him John, and persuade George not to let his partiality for me come across. 'Tis a bad name, and goes against a man. If my name had been Edmund, I should have been more fortunate. I was surprised to hear of the state of society at Louisville; it seems you are just as ridiculous there as we are here—threepenny parties, halfpenny dances. The best thing I have heard of is your shooting; for it seems you follow the gun. Give my compliments to Mrs. Audubon, and tell her I cannot think her either good-looking or honest. Tell Mr. Audubon he's a fool, and Briggs that 'tis well I was not Mr. A——.

Saturday, Jan 15th.

It is strange that George, having to stop so short a time in England, I should not have seen him for nearly two days. He has been to Haslam's, and does not encourage me to follow his example. He had given promise to dine with the same party tomorrow, but has sent an excuse which I am glad of, as we shall have a pleasant party with us tomorrow. We expect Charles here today. This is a beautiful day. I hope you will not quarrel with it if I call it an American one. The sun comes upon the snow and makes a prettier candy than we have on twelfth-night cakes. George is busy this morning in making copies of my verses. He is making one now of an Ode to the Nightingale which is like reading an account of the Black Hole at Calcutta on an ice-bergh. You will say this is a matter of course. I am glad it is—I mean that I should like your brothers more the more I know them. I should spend much more time with them if our lives were more run in parallel; but we can talk but on one subject—that is you.

The next interpolation follows the passage about the Irish servant who said Keats's portrait of Shakespeare was like her father, " only he had more colour than the engraving" (page 54, Volume IV) :—

You will find on George's return that I have not been neglecting your affairs. The delay was unfortunate, not faulty. Perhaps by this time you have received my three last letters, not one of which had reach'd before George sail'd. I would give two-pence to have been over the world as much as he has. I wish I had money enough to do nothing but travel about for years.

After the allusion to the ladies to whom Keats was afraid to speak "for fear of some sickly reiteration of phrase or sentiment," also at page 54, Mr. Speed adds :—

When they were at the dance the other night I tried manfully to sit near and talk to them, but to no purpose; and if I had I [sic] would have been to no purpose still. My question or observation must have been an old one, and the rejoinder very antique indeed.

After the words " I shall enjoy cities more" (Volume IV, page 55) the American edition gives the following passage, obviously a rejoinder to some strictures of Mrs. George Keats's on American ladies :—

If the American ladies are worse than the English, they must be very bad. You say you should like your

Emily brought up here. You had better bring her up yourself. You know a good number of English ladies; what encomium could you give of half a dozen of them? The greater part seem to me downright American. I have known more than one Mrs. Audubon. Her affectation of fashion and politeness cannot transcend ours. Look at our Cheapside tradesmen's sons and daughters —only fit to be taken off by a plague. I hope now soon to come to the time when I shall never be forced to walk through the city and hate as I walk.

After this, and before the account of the three witty people[1] *(also at page* 55*) we find the following in Mr. Speed's version :—*

Monday, Jan. 17

George had a quick rejoinder to his letter of excuse to Haslam, so we had not his company yesterday, which I was sorry for, as there was our old set.

Between the account of the three wits and the " three people of no wit at all" (foot of page 55, *Volume IV), Mr. Speed gives the following passage :—*

Charles came on Saturday, but went early; he seems to have schemes and plans, and wants to get off. He is quite right; I am glad to see him employed at business. You remember I wrote you a story about a woman

---

[1] To the paragraph about Rice, Reynolds, and Richards Mr. Speed adds, after the words "The first is Swiftean, the second Tom Cribean, the third Shandean," the words, "And yet these three eaus are not three eaus but one eau." This is nonsense: what Keats wrote was, of course, "And yet these three eans are not three eans but one ean," meaning that, although there is a distinction between the wit of Swift, of Tom Moore (as exemplified in *Tom Crib's Memorial to Congress*), and of Sterne in *Tristram Shandy*, the essential quality of the wit is the same in all three.

named Alice[1] being made young again, or some such stuff. In your next letter tell me whether I gave it as my own, or whether I gave it as a matter Brown was employed upon at the time. He read it over to George the other day, and George said he had heard it all before. So Brown suspects I have been giving you his story as my own. I should like to set him right in it by your evidence. George has not returned from town; when he does I shall tax his memory. We had a young, long, raw, lean Scotchman with us yesterday, call'd Thornton. Rice, for fun or for mistake, would persist in calling him Stevenson.

The last and perhaps best interpolation of the American editor comes after the words " Young lambs to sell" on page 56 of Volume IV,—to the exclusion of three lines about "pickings in George's letters about the prairie settlements," which, as the reader has already seen, Mr. Speed introduces elsewhere (page 169, ante). The fresh passage, which probably preceded immediately the "new departure" of "Friday 27th" which Mr. Speed rejects, is as follows:—

Twang-dillo-dee. This, you must know, is the amen to nonsense. I know a good many places where amen should be scratched out, rubbed over with po[u]nce made of Momus's little finger bones, and in its place Twang-dillo-dee written. This is the word I shall be tempted to write at the end of most modern poems. Every American book ought to have it. It would be a good distinction in society. My Lords Wellington and Castlereagh, and Canning, and many more, would do well to wear Twang-dillo-dee written on their backs,

---

[1] Presumably the name of the old woman referred to in the long interpolated passage about a story of Brown's (see pages 126-7).

instead of wearing ribbons in their button-holes. How many people would go sideways along walls and quickset hedges to keep their Twang-dillo-dee out of sight, or wear large pigtails to hide it. However, there would be so many that the Twang-dillo-dees would keep one another in countenance—which Brown cannot do for me. I have fallen away lately. Thieves and murderers would gain rank in the world, for would any one of them have the poorness of spirit to condescend to be a Twang-dillo-dee? "I have robbed many a dwelling-house; I have killed many a fowl, many a goose, and many a Man (would such gentlemen say), but, thank heaven, I was never yet a Twang-dillo-dee." Some philosophers in the moon, who spy at our globe as we do at theirs, say that Twang-dillo-dee is written in large letters on our globe of earth; they say the beginning of the "T" is just on the spot where London stands, London being built within the flourish; "wan" reaches downwards and slants as far as Timbuctoo in Africa; the tail of the "g" goes slap across the Atlantic into the Rio della Plata; the remainder of the letters wrap around New Holland, and the last "e" terminates in land we have not yet discovered. However, I must be silent; these are dangerous times to libel a man in—much more a world.

The document printed at pages xxx *and* xxxi *of the first volume of this edition, and mentioned as having been intended to serve as Keats's last will and testament, has received a full authentication since* 1883. *In was in fact sent in a letter to Keats's friend and publisher John Taylor, whose nephew, Mr. John Taylor, has found it apart from the documents which he placed at my disposal when I was at work on these volumes as issued in* 1883. *The testa-*

mentary writing was not quite complete or perfectly accurate as printed from the transcript lent to me by Sir Charles Dilke; and I now give it from the original with the covering letter to Taylor :—

Wentworth Place

My dear Taylor

I do not think I mentioned anything of a Passage to Leghorn by Sea. Will you join that to your enquiries, and, if you can, give a peep at the Birth [*sic*] if the Vessel is [in] our river.

Your sincere friend
John Keats

P.S. Somehow a copy of Chapman's Homer, lent to me by Haydon, has disappeared from my Lodgings—it has quite flown I am affraid [*sic*], and Haydon urges the return of it so that I must get one at Longman's and send it to Lisson Grove—or you must—or as I have given you a job on the River—ask Mistessey.[1] I had written a Note to this effect to Hessey some time since but crumpled it up in hopes that the Book might come to light. This morning Haydon has sent another messenger. The copy was in good condition with the head. Damn all thieves! Tell Woodhouse I have not lost his Blackwood.

Mr. Taylor endorsed the letter as follows :—

"*Inclosed in this Letter I received a Testamentary Paper in John Keats's Handwriting without date on which I have endorsed a memorandum to this effect for the purpose of identifying it & for better security it is hereunto annexed.*

John Taylor"

22 *Sept* 1820

---

[1] Meant, of course, to indicate Mr. Hessey.

The " Testamentary Paper" runs thus :—

My Chest of Books divide among my friends.

In case of my death this scrap of paper may be serviceable in your possession.

All my Estate real and personal consists in the hopes of the sale of books publish'd or unpublish'd. Now I wish *Brown* and you to be the first paid Creditors—the rest is in nubibus—but in case it should shower pay my Taylor the few pounds I owe him.

This memorandum, again, is thus endorsed in the handwriting of the recipient :—

" *N.B. On the* 14*th August or the* 15*th* 1820 *I received this paper which is in John Keats's Handwriting inclosed in the annexed Letter which came by the* 3^d *post.*

John Taylor"

22 *Sept* 1820

" *The Philosophy of Mystery," by Walter Cooper Dendy* (1841), *yields a morsel by Keats with which I was not acquainted in* 1883. *Treating of " Poetic Phantasy, or Frenzy" (page* 99), *the writer says—*" *Even in the lecture-room of Saint Thomas's, I have seen Keats in a deep poetic dream : his mind was on Parnassus with the muses. And here is a quaint fragment which he one evening scribbled in our presence, while the precepts of Sir Astley Cooper fell unheeded on his ear :—"*

Whenne Alexandre the Conqueroure was wayfayringe in ye londe of Inde, there mette hym a damoselle of marveillouse beautie slepynge uponne the herbys and flourys. He colde ne loke uponne her withouten grete plesance, and he was welle nighe loste in wondrement. Her forme was everyche whytte lyke ye fayrest carvynge of Quene Cythere, onlie thatte y^t was swellyd and blushyd wyth warmthe and lyffe wythalle.

Her forhed was as whytte as ys the snowe whyche ye talle hed of a Norwegian pyne stelythe from ye northerne wynde. One of her fayre hondes was yplaced thereonne, and thus whytte wyth whytte was ymyngld as ye gode Arthure saythe, lyke whytest lylys yspredde on whyttest snowe; and her bryghte eyne whenne she them oped, sparklyd lyke Hesperus through an evenynge cloude.

Theye were yclosyd yn slepe, save that two slauntynge raies shotte to her mouthe, and were theyre bathyd yn sweetenesse, as whenne bye chaunce ye moone fyndeth a banke of violettes and droppethe thereonne ye sylverie dewe.

The authoure was goynge onne withouthen descrybynge ye ladye's breste, whenne lo, a genyus appearyd— "Cuthberte," sayeth he, "an thou canst not descrybe ye ladye's breste, and fynde a simile thereunto, I forbyde thee to proceede yn thy romaunt." Thys, I kennd fulle welle, far surpassyd my feble powres, and forthwythe I was fayne to droppe my quille.

Although this is a sufficiently boyish piece of trifling, it is not quite what any boy might have written, and is in some respects characteristic. It has not, of course, any connexion with the study of Chatterton, but is interesting as evidence that Sir John Mandeville must be reckoned among the sources of Keats's English.

This place must serve for the introduction of one more item—a piece of contemporary testimony. Dr. R. Garnett informs me that his father was intimately acquainted with Joseph Ritchie the African traveller, who is mentioned by Haydon (Volume IV, page 356) as having promised Keats to carry "Endymion" to Africa with him and fling it into the midst of the Sahara Desert.[1] *In a letter to Mr. Garnett written in 1818, Ritchie says—"If you have not seen the poems of J. Keats, a lad of about 20, they are well worth your reading. If I am not mistaken, he is to be the great poetical luminary of the age to come." Had Keats lived, Ritchie might not have been far wrong.*

---

[1] See page 79, foot-note, and also page 114, where Keats refers to this matter.

ADDENDA.

ADDENDA.

HAVING recently had an opportunity of visiting Teignmouth, I made further enquiries about the brooks mentioned by Keats as Arch Brook and Larch Brook, in the poem called *Teignmouth* which appears at pages 260-3 of the second volume of the Library Edition. Arch Brook, or Archy Brook, falls into the Teign on the Shaldon side just below Coomb Cellars: the road passes across it by means of a single arch. Of Larch Brook "the oldest inhabitant" can tell me nothing: probably Keats chose to give that name either to the Bitton (Coomb Vale) brook or to the Brimley brook, for the sake of the jingle.

Since these sheets came from the press, my son Maurice Buxton Forman has found in the catalogue of a New York autograph auction the following extract from a letter addressed by Keats to an unnamed correspondent:—

"If George succeeds it will be better, certainly, that they should stop in America; if not, why not return?

It is better in ill luck to have at least the comfort of one's friends than to be shipwrecked among Americans. But I have good hopes, as far as I can judge from what I have heard from George. He should by this time be taught alertness and carefulness. If they should stop in America for five or six years let us hope they may have about three children. Then the eldest will be getting old enough to be society. The very crying will keep their ears employed and their spirits from being melancholy."

It is scarcely to be doubted that the extract represents a genuine letter of Keats, and that an interesting one. The following is unquestionably genuine, and is given from the original letter, addressed outside to "Mr. William Haslam, Frampton & Co., Leadenhall Street":

My dear Haslam,

We have news at last—and tolerably good—they have not gone to the Settlement—they are both in good Health—I read the letter to Mrs. Wylie to day and requested her after her Sons had read it—they would enclose it to you immediately which was faithfully promised. Send it me like Lightning that I may take it to Walthamstow.

Yours ever and amen
John Keats

Though it has no heading or written date, the letter

is legibly post-marked "Hampstead" and "12 o'clock MY. 13 1819," and is clearly one of the letters which Keats told his sister he was writing to friends when he wrote to her on this occasion (Volume III, page 300). It bears a black seal, the device of which is a lyre with the motto "Qui me néglige me désole." Haslam, as may be seen at page 301 of Volume III, prevented Keats from reading the letter to his sister at Walthamstow, by tearing it into small pieces. The reason for this act is still to seek; there is nothing to account for it in Keats's letter.

In Medwin's Life of Shelley (1847) occur some interesting passages about Keats, including certain extracts from a letter which seemed to be from Fanny Brawne. From the lady's family I learnt in 1877 that Medwin's mysteriously introduced correspondent was no other than she. Indeed, I had actually cut out the relative portion of his book for use in the introduction to the *Letters of John Keats to Fanny Brawne*. By some inexplicable oversight I omitted even to refer to Medwin and the passages in question; and they remained for Professor Colvin to point out in his "English Men of Letters" *Keats*. I now gladly follow Mr. Colvin's lead in citing an important authority upon the vexed question of Fanny Brawne's appreciation of Keats. The following is what Medwin gives from her communication as bearing upon the effect of the *Quarterly Review* article on Keats:

"I did not know Keats at the time the review appeared. It was published, if I remember rightly, in June, 1818.[1] However great his mortification might have been, he was not, I should say, of a character likely to have displayed it in the manner mentioned in Mrs. Shelley's Remains of her husband. Keats, soon after the appearance of the review in question, started on a walking expedition into the Highlands. From thence he was forced to return, in consequence of the illness of a brother, whose death a few months afterwards affected him strongly.

"It was about this time that I became acquainted with Keats. We met frequently at the house of a mutual friend, (not Leigh Hunt's), but neither then nor afterwards did I see anything in his manner to give the idea that he was brooding over any secret grief or disappointment. His conversation was in the highest degree interesting, and his spirits good, excepting at moments when anxiety regarding his brother's health dejected them. His own illness, that commenced in January 1820, began from inflammation in the lungs, from cold. In coughing, he ruptured a blood-vessel. An hereditary tendency to consumption was aggravated by the excessive susceptibility of his temperament, for I never see those often quoted lines of Dryden without

---

[1] It appeared in No. XXXVII, headed "April, 1818," on page 1, but described on the wrapper as "published in September, 1818."

thinking how exactly they applied to Keats:—

> The fiery soul, that working out its way,
> Fretted the pigmy body to decay.

From the commencement of his malady he was forbidden to write a line of poetry, and his failing health, joined to the uncertainty of his prospects, often threw him into deep melancholy.

"The letter, p. 295 of Shelley's Remains, from Mr. Finch, seems calculated to give a very false idea of Keats. That his sensibility was most acute, is true, and his passions were very strong, but not violent, if by that term violence of temper is implied. His was no doubt susceptible, but his anger seemed rather to turn on himself than on others, and in moments of greatest irritation, it was only by a sort of savage despondency that he sometimes grieved and wounded his friends. Violence such as the letter describes, was quite foreign to his nature. For more than a twelvemonth before quitting England, I saw him every day, often witnessed his sufferings, both mental and bodily, and I do not hesitate to say that he never could have addressed an unkind expression, much less a violent one, to any human being. During the last few months before leaving his native country, his mind underwent a fierce conflict; for whatever in moments of grief or disappointment he might say or think, his most ardent desire was to live to redeem his name from the obloquy cast upon it; nor was it till he knew his death inevitable, that he eagerly wished to die. Mr. Finch's letter goes on to say—'Keats might be judged insane'—I believe the fever that consumed him, might have brought on a temporary species of delirium that made his friend Mr. Severn's task a painful one."

I must here record with sincere regret the death of my friend Señora Fanny Keats de Llanos, Keats's only sister. This took place at Madrid, after a very short illness, on the 16th of December 1889. Señora Llanos was eighty-six years of age.

INDEX.

INDEX.

Abbey (Mrs.), 82, 113
Abbey (Richard), "does not overstock" the Keatses with money, 80
    Objects to Keats's visits to Fanny Keats, 86
    Referred to, 162, 163, 164
African Kingdom, supposed discovery of an, 120
"After dark vapors," date of Sonnet beginning, 21
ALTHAM AND HIS WIFE, a novel by Charles Ollier, 112
Andrews (Miss), 169
Arch Brook, identified, 181
Archer, his "abominable behaviour" to Miss Mathew, 119-20
    Referred to, 106
Audubon (John James), accused of dishonesty, 157, 162
    Referred to, 170
Audubon (Mrs.), 170, 172
"Authorizing" with Brown, 126

Bailey (Benjamin), Letter from Hampstead to, 72-5
    Passage restored to letter to, 75-6
    An inconstant lover, 131-2
    Referred to, 23, 82, 91, 94, 95
"Bards of Passion and of Mirth," copied into journal-letter of 1818-19, 16, 119
Barnes (Miss), 139
Beattie (James), Keats sees "nothing or weakness" in, 115
Beaumont and Fletcher, Keats reads THE MAID'S TRAGEDY by, 135
Bedhampton, visit of Keats to, 128
    Visit of Brown to, 157
BELLE DAME SANS MERCI (LA), Keats's jocular note on, 151
    Variations shown by holograph of, 35-8
Bentley (Benjamin), 125

Bentley (Mrs.), her noisy children, 73
    Regrets at leaving, 110
    Referred to, 125, 143
Bewick (Wllliam), 85, 144
Birkbeck (Morris), 110, 123, 133
Birkbeck (young), 143, 155
Birthday, Keats's, 103
Blackwood's Magazine, letters belonging to Martin printed in, 109
Brawne (Fanny), described by Keats as beautiful, elegant, graceful, silly, fashionable and strange, 107
    Her estimate of Keats, 184-6
    An occasional " chat and tiff" with, 124
    Referred to, 111
Brawne (Mrs.), still resident at Hampstead, 107
    Referred to, 116, 126, 131, 143
Briggs (—), 170
Brown (Charles Armitage), account of a story by, 126-7, 130
    Generous and friendly actions to Keats, 141
    Referred to, 19, 20, 29, 34, 38, 42, 73, 75, 79, 85, 99, 104, 106, 110, 111, 113, 124, 128, 144, 147, 148, 155, 156, 157, 160, 161, 164, 165, 166, 173, 176
Brown (John), 148
Brown (Mrs. Septimus), 124
Bucke (Charles), quarrel with Kean, 146
Buffon, 141, 142
Burns (Robert), his disposition Southern, 93
Burton's ANATOMY OF MELANCHOLY, Extract from, 158-9
Butler (—), 116
Byron (Lord), a "literary king," 113
    Sale of his works, 128
    " Cuts a figure but is not figurative," 132
    " Byron piping-hot," 145 (*note*)
    Referred to, 73, 124, 145

CALEB WILLIAMS contrasted with WAVERLEY, 118
Capper and Hazlewood, 100, 102
Card-party (a), 149
Cards, Keats wins £10 at, 81
Carlile (Richard), taken to Newgate for issuing *The Deist*, 128
Cats (Mrs. Dilke's), curious behaviour of, 121
Century Guild Hobby Horse (*The*), " fac-simile " of manuscript in, 25
Champion (*The*), Sonnet published in, 22
    Theatrical notices by Keats in, 55-63

Charlotte (Princess), commemoration medal on death of, 82
    Referred to, 108
Chatterton (Thomas), 177
Chaucer (Geoffrey), 135
Chichester, Keats's visit to, 103, 123-4
" Claret feast " (a), 148
Clarke (Charles Cowden), 125
Clergy, Keats's opinion of the, 129
Cobbett (William), gets "a good character" in *The Examiner*, 120
    Referred to, 130
Coleridge (Samuel Taylor), discourses to Keats, 147
Colvin (Professor Sidney), 3, 5, 14, 17, 19, 28, 31, 36, 38, 67, 95, 166, 183
Concert (a), 77
Consecration of a chapel, 128-9
Crabbe (George), 141
Cripps (—), 73, 76, 82, 85, 88

Davenport (Mr.), 127, 144
Davenports (the) of Church Row, 139
Dendy (Walter Cooper), piece of Keats's prose preserved by, 176-7
Dennet (Miss), Columbine at Covent Garden, 79
De Wint (Peter), message to, 93
Dilke (Charles Wentworth), Keats's friendship with, 79
    Sends a farce to Covent Garden, 79
    Keats goes to a dance at house of, 84
    Up to his ears in Walpole's letters, 119
    Removal to Westminster, 130, 144, 145
    His preoccupation about his son, 146
    Referred to, 97, 99, 104, 111, 113, 116, 117, 124, 148
Dilke (Mrs.), "a battle with celery stalks" between Keats and, 122
    Her illness, 97
    Referred to, 69, 79, 105, 113, 116, 121, 131, 146, 169
Dilke (Sir Charles Wentworth), first baronet, son of the above, birthday of, 130
Dilke (Mr.) of Chichester, visit of Keats to, 124
Doeg (Mr. W. H.), 20
DON GIOVANNI, a Pantomime, noticed by Keats in *The Champion*, 61-3, 76-7
Drewe family, a misfortune in the, 113
DREAM (A) AFTER READING DANTE'S EPISODE OF PAULO AND FRANCESCA, date of Sonnet, 29
Drive (a) " behind a leaden horse," 128

Dryden (John), 184
" Duchess of Dunghill (the)," 94

Elliston (Robert William), wishes to put off OTHO THE GREAT, 165
ENDYMION, a test of Keats's imagination, 74
 Second Book copied, 88
 Third Book copied and fourth begun, 90
 Taken to Africa by Ritchie, 114
 A copy bound for Mrs. Reynolds, 93, 94
EVE OF ST. AGNES (THE), Mr. Colvin's collation of Woodhouse's transcript, 5, 14-15
 See ST. AGNES' EVE
Examiner (*The*), LINES WRITTEN IN THE HIGHLANDS printed in, 26
 PETER BELL, A LYRICAL BALLAD, reviewed by Keats in, 48
EXTEMPORE (AN), fresh nonsense verses, 31-4

FAME (SONNETS ON), sent to George and Georgiana Keats, 156
 Variations in, 34-5
FANCY, poem of 1819 sent to George and Georgiana Keats, 117
 Variations of text in, 16
Fielding (Henry), quotation from, 80
 Referred to, 115
Finch (Mr.), " false idea of Keats " given to Shelley by, 185
" Fool Lacon Esqre.," 168
Forman (Maurice Buxton), extract from letter of Keats found by, 181
Fox (George), 127
Framptons (the), 143, 182
Frogley (Miss), Woodhouse's cousin, 108

Garnett (Dr. Richard), 177
Gattie (—), 112
Gifford (William), classified by Brown among " nuisances," 127
 Extracts from Hazlitt's LETTER to, 133-9
Gleig (the Rev. G. R.), 75, 131
Gleig (Miss), Bailey's engagement to, 131-2
Godwin (William), his MANDEVILLE reviewed by Shelley, 80 (*note*)
 Hazlitt's remarks on his ST. LEON, 118-19
Green (Mr.), demonstrator at Guy's, 147
Grover (Miss), 168

INDEX.

"Hadst thou liv'd in days of old," cancelled passages of, 4
Harris (Bob), 79
Hart (Mr.), 169
Haslam (William), new letter to, 182
    Death of his father, 143
    His innamorata, 168
    Referred to, 82, 85, 100, 102, 105, 112, 117, 121, 125, 131, 136, 170, 172
Hastings, adventure with a lady whom Keats met at, 101
Haydon (Benjamin Robert), unpleasantness between Hunt and, 73, 83
    Quarrels with Reynolds, 83
    Keats's Sunday evening with, 79
    Impeded in his work by bad eyes, 97
    Out at elbows, 125
    Referred to, 75, 99, 100, 105, 106, 110, 112, 114, 144, 169, 175
Hazlitt (William), met by Keats at Haydon's, 85
    "Going to play Rackets," 101
    Keats calls on him, 106
    Remarks on Godwin's ST. LEON by, 118-19
    Extracts from his LETTER TO GIFFORD, 133-9
    Referred to, 68, 112, 113 (*note*), 141
Hazlitt (Mrs.) and her son, 124-5
Heart (the), the Mind's Bible, 154
Hessey (James Augustus), 93, 99, 175
Hilton (William), R.A., message to, 93
    Referred to, 144
Hobhouse, letter in *The Examiner* on, 120
Hogarth (William), 115
Holts (the), 124
Hone (William), subscriptions for, 80
Hopner (young), recounts polar adventures with Captain Ross, 105
Horwood (Mr.), 25
Houghton (Lord), Keats collection of, 5
    Referred to, 27, 36, 38, 41, 42, 67, 72, 75, 76, 79 (*note*), 81 (*note*), 85, 87, 88, 90, 91, 93, 95, 114, 122, 123, 142
HUMAN SEASONS (THE), Sonnet, new version of, 23
Hunt (James Henry Leigh), alleged "patronage" of Keats, 73
    Unpleasantness with Haydon, 73, 83
    His LITERARY POCKET-BOOK "sickening stuff," 106
    Strictures on, 109
    Going on badly in money matters, 125
    Referred to, 36, 72, 75, 80, 99, 100, 106, 112, 140, 142, 144, 149, 150, 184
Hunt (Mrs. James Henry Leigh), 80

Hunt (John), 106
HYMN TO APOLLO, new readings, 21
HYPERION, Mr. Colvin's collation of Woodhouse's copy, 5, 17-19
    Last line recovered, 19
HYPERION, A VISION, an attempt to reconstruct the poem, 19

" I had a dove," song of 1819 sent to George and Georgiana Keats, 119
    New readings for, 26
Imagination, powers of the, 115
Immortality, Keats's opinion on, 104
ISABELLA, transcript by Woodhouse revised by Keats, 10
    Cancelled passages and new readings, 10-14
    Written at Teignmouth, at Reynolds's suggestion, 14

Jeffrey (Mr.), 76, 81 (*note*), 95, 122, 123, 139, 142
Jennings (Mrs.), threatens a chancery suit, 164
Jesus and Socrates compared, 142

Kean (Edmund), in Howard Payne's BRUTUS, 106
    His quarrel with Mr. Bucke, 146
    Referred to, 58, 133, 156, 169
Keasle (Miss), 97, 104, 161
Keasle (Mr. and Mrs.), 195
Keats (Emily), 172
Keats (Fanny), 75, 82, 86, 95, 98, 105, 112, 113, 136, 183, 186
KEATS (GEORGE), variations in EPISTLE TO, 4
    Valentine written for, 4
    Referred to, 15, 16, 26, 35, 67, 69, 74, 94, 95, 166, 167, 168, 169, 170, 171, 182
Keats (George and Georgiana), new passages of letter to, 96-103
    Fresh passages of letter of 1818-19 to, 104-22
    Additions to letter begun 14 February 1819 to, 123-156
    Additions to Winchester journal-letter to, 157-64
Keats (George and Thomas), new letter to, 76-82
    New passages of letter to, 85-7
Keats (Georgiana Augusta), additions to letter to, 166
    Referred to, 15, 16, 26, 102, 182
    See Wylie (Georgiana Augusta)
Keats (Thomas), Junior, his view as to immortality, 104
    Wells's cruel hoax on, 144, 148
    Referred to, 69, 92, 96, 98, 101, 102, 103, 184

Kemble (Charles), 56, 57, 113
Kent (Bessie), Keats attributes an article by Shelley to, 80
KING STEPHEN, manuscript variations, 38-42
KING LEAR, SONNET ON SITTING DOWN TO READ (1818), variation in, 25
Kingston (—), 78, 79
Kirkman (—), beaten and robbed in Pond Street, 106
    His family badly off, 119
        "Villainous trick" of his "Uncle William," 119
        Referred to, 121
Knox (John), 127
Kotzebue (August von), assassination of, 146

"Lacon (Fool) Esqre.," 168
Lamb (Charles), tipsy at Haydon's, 79
    Referred to, 106
LAMIA, ISABELLA, THE EVE OF ST. AGNES, AND OTHER POEMS, fresh collations, 5-19
    A rejected title-page, 5
LAMIA, cancelled passages and readings from fragment of draft, 6-9
Landor (Walter Savage), his lines TO RECRUITS a tribute to Keats, 145 (*note*)
Landseer, 79
Leicester (Sir John), Keats visits gallery of, 144
Lewis (Mr.), calls Keats "quite the little poet," 126
    Kind to Tom Keats, 98-9
    Referred to, 105, 130
LINES ON THE MERMAID TAVERN, Woodhouse's transcript, 17
LINES ON SEEING A LOCK OF MILTON'S HAIR, newly found draft, 23-4
LINES WRITTEN IN THE SCOTCH HIGHLANDS, printed in *The Examiner*, 26
    Partly printed in *The New Monthly Magazine*, 27
    Variations shown by holograph, 27-8
Liston (John), 113
"Literary kings," Scott and Byron described as, 113
Llanos (Señora), *See* Keats (Fanny)
London Coffee House, Keats goes to a dance at, 84

Macmillan's Magazine, Article by Mr. Colvin in, 31, 36
Macready (William Charles), 56

MAID'S TRAGEDY (THE), Keats reads, 135
Man formed by circumstances, 155
Mancur (—), 148
Mandeville (Sir John), among the sources of Keats's English, 177
Manker = Mancur? 119
Martin (John), 90, 109, 148, 151
Martin (Miss), Bailey's attentions to, 131
Maw ("the Apostate"), tragedy by, 125
Mathew (Caroline), "abominable behaviour" of Archer to, 119-20
Matthews (Charles), 160
Medwin (Thomas), extract from Life of Shelley by, 184-6
Mermaid Tavern, *See* LINES
Millar (Miss), her birthday dance, 107, 125
    Referred to, 104, 122, 149, 161
Millar (Mrs.), 96, 97, 98, 100, 149
Milton, *See* LINES and PARADISE LOST
Monkhouse (Mr.), 79, 136
Moore (Thomas), Hunt invites Keats to meet, 109
    Dinner given in Dublin to, 116
    "Nothing in" his TOM CRIB'S MEMORIAL TO CONGRESS, 135
    Referred to, 140
Murray (John), 128 (*note*)

NEHEMIAH MUGGS, manuscript lent by Horace Smith to Keats, 89
Neville (Henry), house surgeon to Princess Charlotte, 108
New Monthly Magazine (The), part of LINES WRITTEN IN THE HIGHLANDS given in, 27
Northcote, 144
Novello's, Keats and Brown's sufferings at, 106, 109
Novello (Mrs.), 112

ODE TO A NIGHTINGALE, Woodhouse's transcript of, 15
ODE TO PSYCHE, in holograph of journal-letter, February-May 1819, 15
    Variations, 15-16
Ollier (Charles), 100, 112, 126
O'Neill (Miss), 56, 57, 58
OTHO THE GREAT, Elliston *versus* Macready, 165
    Rejected at Drury Lane and offered to Covent Garden, 169
Otway (Thomas), 57
Oxford, fresh particulars as to nonsense verses on, 42-4

Panorama of ships at North Pole, Keats visits, 151
PARADISE LOST, 55
Parson (the), "the black badger with tri-cornered hat," 141
Parsons, Keats's views on, 129
Payne (Howard), Keats sees his tragedy BRUTUS acted, 106
Peachey (—), 107, 123, 133
Peachey family (the), 78
Perfectibility, Keats's views as to, 152
PETER BELL, by Wordsworth, travestied by Reynolds, 48-52, 145
PETER BELL, A LYRICAL BALLAD, reviewed by Keats in *The Examiner*, 48-52, 149-50
PHILOSOPHY OF MYSTERY (THE), fragment of Keats's prose from, 176-7
"Petition to the Governors of St. Luke," 140
Pindar (Peter), Severn drinks the health of, 78
Pizarro, 152
POEMS (1817), fresh collations, 3-5
Porter (Jane), borrows ENDYMION and desires Keats's acquaintance, 107-8
    Tragedy by, 125

Quarterly Review article, effect on Keats of, 183-4

Radcliffe (Ann), 55
Redhall (Mr.), parties given by, 81, 111
    Referred to, 116
RETRIBUTION, OR THE CHIEFTAIN'S DAUGHTER, a Tragedy, noticed by Keats in *The Champion*, 55-8, 76-7
Reynolds (Mrs. Charlotte), copy of ENDYMION to be bound for, 93, 94
    Referred to, 131
Reynolds (Jane), letters from Oxford to her and Mariane, 69-72
    Referred to, 69, 72, 77
Reynolds (John Hamilton), Sonnet to Keats by, 45
    Review by Keats of his PETER BELL, 49-52
    New letter to, 68
    Fresh passages of letters to, 69, 87-8, 91-2, 94
    Quarrel between Haydon and, 83
    Serious illness of, 89, 90
    "Become an Edinburgh Reviewer," 106
    Referred to, 14, 17, 42, 72, 73, 75, 76, 83, 85, 88, 101, 113, 125, 130, 143, 148, 149, 151

Reynolds (Mariane), letters from Oxford to her and Jane, 69-72
    Bailey's inconstancy to, 131
    Referred to, 71, 77
Rice (James), fresh passage in letter to, 90
    Fresh letter to, 164-6
    His illness, 73, 86
    Abandons Bailey, 132
    Referred to, 76, 78, 81, 91, 99, 113, 125, 130, 151, 173
Richards, 125, 146
Richardson (Samuel), 144
Ritchie (Joseph), meets Keats at Haydon's, 79
    News from Tripoli of, 114
    Foretells Keats's greatness, 178
Robertson's AMERICA, Keats reads, 152
ROBIN HOOD, variation in Woodhouse's transcript of, 17
Robinson (Miss), obnoxious to Keats, 111
ROBINSON CRUSOE, among the sources of Keats's English, 167
Rogers (Samuel), a poem "deadborn" from, 124
    Referred to, 140
Rondeau, Keats's conception of the, 119
Ross (Captain), polar expedition of, 105
Rowe (Nicholas), 57

ST. AGNES' EVE, written at Chichester, 124
Salvation, a "grand system" of, 153
Sawrey, Tom Keats's doctor, gives a rout, 143
    Referred to, 77, 82
Sawrey (Mrs.), 143
Scott (John), visited by Tom Keats in Paris, 79
Scott (Sir Walter), compared with Smollett, 80
    A "literary king," 113
    "Manly Scott," 145 (*note*)
    See WAVERLEY
Severn (Joseph), has typhus fever, 97
    Referred to, 77, 78, 81, 186
Shakespeare, could a "superior being" see "nothing or weakness" in? 115
    "Led a life of Allegory," 132-3
    Gifford misrepresents Hazlitt's views on, 137-8
    Referred to, 136
SHARING EVE'S APPLE, poem sent in a letter to Reynolds, 87
Sheil (Richard Lalor), 140

Shelley (Percy Bysshe), meets Keats at Hunt's or Haydon's, 73
    Keats refuses to visit him, 74-5
    Reviews MANDEVILLE in *The Examiner*, 80
    Medwin's Life quoted, 183-6
Skinner (—), 148
Smith (Horace), tired of Hunt, 73
    Lends Keats manuscript of NEHEMIAH MUGGS, 89
Smollett (Tobias), compared with Scott, 80
Snook (John), visit of Keats to, 110, 124, 125
Snook (John), of Belmont Castle, 128 (*note*)
Snuff, verses on women, wine and, 20
    Keats almost gives it up, 117
Socrates compared with Jesus, 142
    Referred to, 152
SONG OF FOUR FAERIES, new readings for, 30-1
SONNET ON THE SEA, published in *The Champion*, 22
SONNET TO HOMER, new reading in, 23
SONNET TO THE NILE, date of, 25
    New readings in, 25
SONNET ON BLUE, new readings in, 25-6
SONNET TO A LADY SEEN FOR A FEW MOMENTS AT VAUXHALL, date of, 26
SONNET TO SLEEP, holograph of, 35
SONNET TO MRS. REYNOLDS'S CAT, variations in, 44
SONNETS ON FAME, variations shown by holograph of, 34-5
Sonnets, other references to, 21, 22, 23, 25, 29
Sore throat, caught in Mull, 96
    Keats fears to dance on account of, 125
    Other references to, 112, 114, 117, 123
Southcote (Johanna), 127
Southey (Robert), 140
SPENSERIAN STANZAS ON CHARLES ARMITAGE BROWN, variations in, 30
Speed (Mr. J. G.), 67, 76, 78 (*note*), 81 (*note*), 104, 123, 124 (*note*), 125, 128, 157, 158, 159 (*note*), 161, 162, 163, 164 (*note*), 166, 168 (*note*), 171, 172, 173
STAFFA, cancelled passage of, 28-9
Stephens (Henry), 20, 78
Story, a dreadful, 165-6

Tale, Keats proposes to write a, 100
Taylor (Jeremy), 132

Taylor (John), fresh letters to, 83, 88, 92, 103, 156, 175
    Fresh passages of letters to, 90, 91
    Requested to lend Keats £30, 103
    Keats intends to stay with, 125
    Referred to, 12, 28, 99, 142, 143, 149, 151, 168
Teignmouth, ISABELLA written at, 14
    George and Thomas Keats staying at, 76-7
    Fresh enquiries as to brooks at, 181
Terry, 56, 58
Thornton (—), 173
Tighe (Mrs.), Keats sees "nothing or weakness" in, 115
TOM CRIB'S MEMORIAL TO CONGRESS, "nothing in it," 135
Towers (Mr.), 124
Trimmer (Mr.), "an acquaintance of Peachey's," 107
"Twang-dillo-dee, the amen to nonsense," 173
Twiss (Horace), 113

"Unfelt, unheard, unseen," new reading for poem beginning, 21-2

Valentine, "Had'st thou liv'd in days of old" written for a, 4
"Vale of soul-making (the)," 153
Voltaire's SIÈCLE DE LOUIS XIV, Keats reads, 152

Waldegrave (Miss), will Keats dance with her? 107
    "Staid and self-possessed as usual," 125
    Referred to, 97, 149, 158, 163
WAVERLEY contrasted with CALEB WILLIAMS, 118
Way (Mr.), a great Jew-converter, 128
Webb (Mrs.), 124
"Welcome joy, and welcome sorrow," new readings in poem beginning, 22
Wells (Charles), Keats visits theatres with, 84, 86
    Cruel hoax on Tom Keats, 144, 148
    Referred to, 77, 78, 80
Wells (Mrs.), 82
Westminster, Keats thinks of living at, 144, 145
"When I have fears," date of sonnet beginning, 22
    New reading in, 23
"Why did I laugh to-night?"—new readings in sonnet beginning, 29

Will (Keats's), 174-6
Williams (Mr. Dominie), 124
Winchester journal-letter, new passages in, 157-64
Winter (Miss), 139
Women, "inadequacy" of, 115
WOMEN, WINE AND SNUFF, early nonsense verses, 20
Woodhouse (Richard), the Keats Commonplace book of, 4, 5, 10, 14, 15, 17, 19, 21, 22, 25, 26, 28, 29, 44
    Referred to, 67, 72, 92, 93, 95, 103, 107, 124, 149, 151, 175
Wordsworth (William), parodied by Keats, 42-3
    Travestied by Reynolds, 48, 145
    Keats to dine with him, 78
    Keats dines with him and sees him frequently, 83
    In a stiff collar, 78
    At Haydon's, 79
    His egotism and vanity, 89
    Announcement of his PETER BELL, 145
    Referred to, 73, 85, 141, 150
World (the), "the vale of soul-making," 153
Wylie (Charles), 96, 100, 104, 143, 158, 168, 170, 182
Wylie (Henry), 97, 98, 100, 125, 140, 143, 155, 158, 170, 182
Wylie (Georgiana Augusta), Valentine sent to, 4
Wylie (Mrs.), 95, 96, 100, 104, 107, 129, 144, 149, 155, 158, 168, 170, 182
Wylie (Mrs. Henry), 168

Yellow Dwarf (*The*), Reynolds's Robin Hood sonnets in, 17
Young (Charles Mayne), 56, 57

THE END.